RISE OF A DYNASTY

RISE
OF A
DYNASTY

The '57 Celtics, the First Banner, and
the Dawning of a New America

BILL REYNOLDS

 NEW AMERICAN LIBRARY

NEW AMERICAN LIBRARY
Published by New American Library,
a division of Penguin Group (USA) Inc.,
375 Hudson Street, New York, New York 10014, USA
Penguin Group (Canada), 90 Eglinton Avenue East, Suite 700, Toronto, Ontario M4P 2Y3,
Canada (a division of Pearson Penguin Canada Inc.) · Penguin Books Ltd., 80 Strand,
London WC2R 0RL, England · Penguin Ireland, 25 St. Stephen's Green, Dublin 2, Ireland
(a division of Penguin Books Ltd.) · Penguin Group (Australia), 250 Camberwell Road,
Camberwell, Victoria 3124, Australia (a division of Pearson Australia Group Pty. Ltd.) ·
Penguin Books India Pvt. Ltd., 11 Community Centre, Panchsheel Park, New Delhi - 10017,
India · Penguin Group (NZ), 67 Apollo Drive, Rosedale, North Shore 0632, New Zealand
(a division of Pearson New Zealand Ltd.) · Penguin Books (South Africa) (Pty.) Ltd.,
24 Sturdee Avenue, Rosebank, Johannesburg 2196, South Africa

Penguin Books Ltd., Registered Offices:
80 Strand, London WC2R 0RL, England

First published by New American Library,
a division of Penguin Group (USA) Inc.

First Printing, November 2010
1   3   5   7   9   10   8   6   4   2

 REGISTERED TRADEMARK—MARCA REGISTRADA

LIBRARY OF CONGRESS CATALOGING-IN-PUBLICATION DATA:
Reynolds, Bill, 1945–
Rise of a dynasty: the '57 Celtics, the first banner, and the
dawning of a new America/Bill Reynolds.
    p.   cm.
ISBN 978-0-451-23135-2
1. Boston Celtics (Basketball team)—History.   2. Basketball—Social aspects—
Massachusetts—Boston.   3. Boston (Mass.)—Race relations—History—20th
century.   4. Racism in sports—United States—History.   5. United States—History—
20th century.   I. Title.
GV885.52.B67R49 2010
796.323'640974461—dc22   2010026729

Set in Fairfield • Designed by Elke Sigal

Printed in the United States of America

To my brother, Geoffrey

RISE OF A DYNASTY

PROLOGUE

I n the spring of 2008, the Celtics were in the NBA Finals, trying to put a seventeenth banner up in the rafters of the TD Banknorth Garden in Boston.

The "Drive for 17."

That had been the slogan that spring, the catchy phrase, as once again Boston and all of New England were caught up in another Celtics play-off run.

It had been twenty-two years since the last one, back when the names had been Larry Bird and Kevin McHale, DJ and Danny Ainge, back when the Celtics in the NBA Finals seemed all but built into the schedule, a rite of spring. It had been more than two decades of the NBA Finals being held in other cities, and during that period the Celtics seemed to drift farther and farther into irrelevancy, overshadowed by both the Red Sox and the Patriots. It was as if their glory days were all in the past tense, those sixteen championship banners up in the rafters, once a symbol of excellence, beginning to stare down like accusers.

The spring of 2008 changed that.

Not only did it resurrect interest in the Celtics; it also resurrected interest in the Celtics' storied history, the one represented by all those banners, the constant reminder of what the Celtics had once been. And as the Celtics got closer and closer to that seventeenth title, the Garden became loud and alive again. The hope was for another great Celtics team for a new generation, with Bird, McHale, and Parish morphing into another Big Three of Kevin Garnett, Paul Pierce, and Ray Allen. You could almost close your eyes and see it as all the same story, one big continuum, one banner no different from another.

But what did they know?

That was the question I asked myself as people flocked to this new Garden, with its earsplitting music and light shows, flashing message boards, and bump-and-grind dancers; such were the accoutrements of today's NBA.

What did they know of that first banner, the one from 1957, the one that had started it all?

For you had to be over age sixty to remember it; you had to have grown up with Ike in the White House and Elvis all over the radio. You had to have come of age in the era of fallout shelters and Sadie Hawkins dances in the gym, back before the Beatles and the Kennedys, before Vietnam and color television, back when social unrest was some kid hot-rodding his car in some quiet suburban neighborhood. You had to have grown up in such a different America, a time when the civil rights movement was still in the future and there were few African-American players in the NBA. It was such a different basketball world.

Even then, you might have been a little late to the dance, too young to remember the early days of the NBA, back when professional basketball had all the glamour of roller derby. Often called a goon's game, it was frequently ignored by both the big-name newspaper columnists, who didn't consider it worth their attention, and by the majority of the American sporting public. The NBA was in only its eleventh year in the spring of '57, that spring that started the Celtics' story.

To many in the new Garden in the spring of 2008, the NBA had started with Larry Bird and Magic Johnson in the late seventies. This was often the historical reference point, the beginning of the modern NBA story. Certainly it was the renewal of the great Celtics-Lakers rivalry. Or else it was Michael Jordan a few years later, the beginning of the glittering world of megasalaries, huge endorsements, and stars who walked across the American sports landscape like young princes. To many in the Garden that spring, what they knew about those first years of the Celtics dynasty, of names like Cousy and Russell, they knew from grainy old newsreels and black-and-white photographs, those remnants of another era. Or they knew them from the message board in the Garden, where the icons of history were periodically flashed up when the Celtics paid homage to their past.

Occasionally, they would still be at the Garden, a visible presence, living history. Cousy had been an analyst on the Celtics television games for years. You couldn't be a Celtics fan without knowing who Bob Cousy was, even if the only time you had seen him play was on an old newsreel; even if you didn't know that once upon a time he'd been called "Mr. Basketball," back in the mid-fifties when he was arguably the biggest name in the game, the flashy guard who threw the ball behind his back and did things on a basketball court that few people had ever done before, one of the players who had made the NBA respectable in an era when so many people in American sport thought it wasn't.

The same was true for Bill Russell, of course, the other mythic figure of the Celtics.

He had been the long-lost Celtic, now back after being away for so long. His time as a Celtic always had been complicated, all the winning and all the titles marred by the prejudice and the discrimination he always had felt in Boston. He was undergoing a certain rebirth, now being called the greatest winner in the history of American sport. There also was the sense, rightly or wrongly, that he had somehow softened, as if most of his battles already had been fought, his demons exorcised. Now he waved to people, laughed his big cackle of a laugh, and to those who had known him in the past, it all seemed incongruous, as though he simply had to be the friendlier twin.

The fans in the Garden had always known Arnold "Red" Auerbach, who passed away in 2006. He'd been a presence at many Celtics game, the old patriarch walking with a cane in those twilight years, always sitting near midcourt across from the benches, about ten rows up. He was regarded as one of the greatest coaches in basketball history, complete with his nine NBA titles to prove it. More important, he was the one constant in the Celtics' long history, as the players came and went, as the eras changed. He had morphed from coach, to general manager, to president, but those were just titles. He *was* the Celtics, a Boston institution right up there with Paul Revere and Fenway Park, Ted Williams and the Kennedys, complete with the statue at Faneuil Hall to prove it.

The Celtics tradition?

In the end, it was Auerbach.

And through the years, as his legend grew and all those championship banners in the rafters kept staring down at fans, his mystique grew, too. The Celtics are down? Red will think of something. The Celtics need a power forward? Don't worry, Red will bamboozle some general manager somewhere. As if regardless of who the Celtics' coach was, or what the names on the door said, Red was really the guy pulling all the strings behind the big curtain; Red was the true wizard.

That had been the perception, and it had remained so until the late nineties, when Rick Pitino became the basketball boss of the Celtics and it became apparent that Auerbach officially was retired, his duties only ceremonial.

By then, Auerbach had long ago become mythic, the fact and the fiction having been sprinkled together for so long, it almost didn't matter what was true and what wasn't. He was revered in ways that would have been unimaginable for many of the sportswriters who had known him when he first came to Boston in 1950. He was revered in ways that would have been unthinkable back in the fifties, back when he'd been trying to carve out a reputation for himself, back when it hadn't always been easy.

The most visible of all the old Celtics in 2008, as the Celtics chased another championship banner, had been Tommy Heinsohn, courtesy of his still being the Celtics' analyst on their television broadcasts. He had been doing it for more than twenty years, and for some inexplicable reason was more popular than ever, an almost lovable figure with his "Tommy points" for hustle, his transformation into this generation's version of Johnny Most.

He was the most comfortable of all the ex-Celtics in those moments when they all were in the spotlight, such as the time during the play-offs in 2002 against the Nets when the four of them, the four who had been such an integral part of that '57 season, had come out on the court before a game. He had been smiling, waving to the crowd, the life of the party. Of all of them, he was the one whose celebrity was still in the present tense, now known more as a broadcaster than for being both a player and a coach. Of all the ex-players, he had sustained the life the longest, and he was still sustaining it through eighty-two games a year.

And when the large crowd cheered them, cheers that were for the great Celtics tradition as well, I would ask myself, What do they know? What do they know about that first banner?

Did they know there had been only one African-American player in the NBA Finals that year?

Did they know the Celtics used to spend several weeks of training camp every fall touring through New England and playing games in all the tank towns as their way of spreading the game and catering to potential fans? Did they know the Celtics did so because they really did have to sell the game then, professional basketball in Boston being too often viewed as almost irrelevant?

Did they know the Celtics always had been a tough sell in Boston, even in 1957, when they were the best team in basketball?

What do they know?

That had been the question I was always asking myself in the spring of 2008 when it became apparent the Celtics were going to beat the Lakers of Kobe Bryant and Phil Jackson and win their seventeenth world title.

What did they know?

Because that first banner had started what we now know as the Celtics basketball story. The Celtics of legend? The Celtics as the greatest dynasty in the history of American sport? It all started in 1957, back in such a different era. It was there, in that long-ago season, that the NBA changed, taking that first big step into being the league we've come to know. In many ways, that was the first season of the modern era, the season when professional basketball took a significant step into the mainstream of American sport.

That is why that first banner is still so significant today, for not only did it change basketball in Boston forever, marking the beginning of the Celtics dynasty, but it also was the beginning of a different sports world in America.

CHAPTER ONE

They rode in together that morning. They rode the thirty miles from Worcester to the Boston Garden to play the biggest game of their lives.

The driver was Bob Cousy, then in his seventh season, as big a name as there was in the National Basketball Association. In the passenger seat was Tom Heinsohn, a rookie with the Boston Celtics. Or maybe it was the other way around—Heinsohn the driver, Cousy the passenger—for neither one remembered now; they remembered only that they always drove in together back then, alternating the driving.

They both lived in Worcester, Cousy because he always had felt comfortable there since leaving Holy Cross in 1950; Heinsohn because he had graduated from Holy Cross the spring before and was working part-time for a Worcester insurance company. Since they both had gone to Holy Cross and were both playing for the Celtics, they would be linked for decades to come, although neither one knew that on this Saturday morning.

It was April 13, 1957.

Ike was in the White House, the police action known as Korea had been over for four years, the hottest singer in the country was a swivel-hipped kid from Mississippi named Elvis Presley, and it often seemed that every kid in America was dancing to something called rock 'n' roll.

They'd been riding together for months now, ever since training camp had started back in October, riding down Route 9 from Worcester to Boston, through Framingham and Natick, through the hills of Newton, and then into Boston. They had done it all year, both for practices and for games, so they certainly were comfortable with each other; yet they were so very different, too.

Cousy already was an established star, often referred to as "Mr. Basketball," a name known to sports fans across the country. He already was being called "the Babe Ruth of basketball," and later would be called the game's first modern player, hyperbole or not. What was not in question, however, was that he was the flashiest player in the game then, the first to throw the ball behind his back, the first to play with the improvisational flair, the sense of individual expression that would come to define basketball. He already had been in the NBA for seven years, in many ways having grown up with it, and now was at the end of the season when he would be the league's MVP, at the very height of his career. Heinsohn was a rookie, his career all ahead of him. Cousy also was seven years older, married with two young daughters, in a different place in his life than the younger Heinsohn, though Heinsohn had been married a month before training camp started.

But it was more than that, too.

They were such different personalities. Cousy was reserved

and driven, both insecure and intense, his emotions so bottled inside of him that he sometimes sleepwalked, his fear of failure the fuel that had propelled him to the top of American sport. Heinsohn was laid-back and comfortable in his own skin, a curious mixture of artist and professional athlete, someone for whom the game had always come easy. Cousy was forever the perfectionist, forever driving both himself and the people around him to do better, whereas Heinsohn seemed to go through life as if always on a clear path to the basket, his adjustment from the college game to the professional game as easy as the transition from high school basketball to college had been for him. Cousy was dark-haired with Gallic features, forever a sense of wariness in his face, like a cardplayer who always kept his cards hidden, while Heinsohn was blond with a brush cut and an open all-American face, the class clown.

This was the undercurrent that seemed to run through their conversations, Cousy the big brother, forever giving advice, forever telling Heinsohn he could be truly great if he only worked at it more, got in better shape, cut back on his smoking; Heinsohn at times chafing at the role that had been assigned to him, the one he had never signed up for. Yet there was also deep affection between them, an affection both shaped and defined by all those rides together.

Or, as Heinsohn once said, "Since Cooz would rather shoot than pass, and since I'd rather shoot than pass, we got along famously."

Heinsohn quickly learned how intense Cousy was, how much he wanted to win; yet he also saw Cousy's dry sense of humor.

"I was the little brother," he said. "Cousy was the captain, the star of the team, the boss man. But he accepted me from the beginning. I think he realized that I could help the team and that I was committed to winning. We became close. It wasn't like we were with each other all the time, because he had roomed with Sharman on the road and continued to do so. But we palled around."

This was to be their last ride of the season, for this was the seventh game of the NBA Finals, the game that would come to define both the Celtics and the NBA, too. They were playing the St. Louis Hawks, an all-white team, while Russell, their African-American rookie center, was the highest profile black player to ever enter the NBA. So in ways that couldn't have been understood on this April morning, the Hawks symbolized what the NBA had been, whereas the Celtics symbolized what the NBA would become. Russell was just the first of the black superstars who would enter the NBA in the late fifties and early sixties. Elgin Baylor, Wilt Chamberlain, and Oscar Robertson would join him, and each of them would change the game in his own idiosyncratic way, making basketball more of the game we've come to know than the one that was played in 1957. Collectively, they would be one of the windows on a changing America, a country that was going through civil rights demonstrations in the South, a graphic example of a nation about to change. The Hawks were a product of a segregated city, one that would change in the next decade, as the country changed. So the present and the past were on the same scorecard in this afternoon's game, right there with who was going to be the NBA champion in 1957.

And if the NBA would start to change as the result of this game, Russell was one of the advance men, even if no one understood that back then, either.

There had been other African-American basketball players in the NBA before Russell. Three had begun playing in 1950, and twenty-one others had been in the NBA until then, his rookie season. But there had never been one in the NBA remotely like Russell, who had arrived in December '56, direct from leading the United States Olympic team to a gold medal in Melbourne, Australia. In many important ways, he was the Jackie Robinson of professional basketball, even if few people recognized it at the time. He was the man who would go on to change basketball athletically and sociologically, too. His becoming a Celtic was a story in itself, one that spoke to both Auerbach's cunning and the reality of the NBA in the fifties. Russell's changing the game forever was still far in the future, the dots yet to connect, like colors in some impressionist painting no one had so far been able to interpret. Also unknown on this April morning in 1957 was that looking at Russell was like looking at America's future, a future with cultural as well as political roots. Music and sports were arguably as important as civil rights marches in changing white America's attitudes and perceptions about African-Americans, who were called Negroes then.

This, too, had been Russell's first year with the Boston Celtics. He was a young, proud black man on the precipice of change, both personally and as a public figure, in ways that also would have been considered unimaginable just a few years before.

He had arrived at Logan Airport on a gray day in mid-December with his new wife, Rose, who had been his college sweetheart, the daughter of one of his teachers at McClymonds High School in Oakland. It was a cold, slushy day and, by his own admission, he arrived with a certain chip on his shoulder. Wearing a white coat and a dark cap on his head, he was met at the airport by new teammate Bill Sharman, who had been back in Boston on the injured list while the Celtics were on the road. Sharman presented him with a giant key to the city. The words on it were WELCOME TO BOSTON. Also at the airport to meet Russell was Celtics owner Walter Brown. It had been Brown, the fleshy-faced man with a heart as big as the Boston Garden he owned, who quickly endeared himself to Russell by saying that Russell should not be penalized for playing in the Olympics, and that Brown would pay half the money Russell was supposed to forfeit for missing the first part of the season.

The irony was that no one, not even Auerbach, really knew what the Celtics were getting with Russell. There was no scouting of college players then, at least not in any structured sense. The NCAA Tournament wasn't televised. No one on the Celtics had ever seen him play except for Heinsohn, who once had played a college game in Madison Square Garden against him. Heinsohn had never seen a big man with that kind of athletic ability, and he had been telling everyone in Boston that Russell was going to be great, even if few people seemed to hear him. The word was Russell couldn't shoot, was too skinny, and there were people in the NBA who thought he'd be a bust, just another college star whose game didn't translate into the rough-and-tumble NBA. Russell ultimately would be remembered for his politics and his social activism, along with all his incredible accomplishments as a basketball player. He also would become the most controversial sports star in Boston history, a product of a certain time and place to be sure, one of the first African-American athletes who was going to speak out about prejudice and discrimination, even if white America didn't want to hear what he had to say. His relationship with Boston always would be problematic at best. Seven years after he first arrived, he would tell the *Saturday Evening Post* he owed the public nothing, and "since I owe them nothing I will pay them nothing." This was his way of saying he would give his all on the court, but nothing off it, whether that was refusing to sign autographs or refusing to smile and treat fans as if they meant anything to him.

Years later he would call Boston a rigidly segregated city and say he would rather be in jail in Sacramento than be the mayor of Boston.

"If Paul Revere were riding today, it would be for racism," he wrote in the late seventies, in the wake of Boston's busing crisis, the worst in the nation's history. "'The niggers are coming. The niggers are coming,' he'd yell as he galloped through town to warn neighborhoods of busing and black homeowners."

But even in his first year with the Celtics, in that winter and spring of '57, no one knew what to make of Bill Russell.

"We were never unfriendly," Cousy would later say of Russell. "I think my shyness prevented us from being closer. It made me gun-shy. Given my situation, the fact that I was the veteran, the captain, I should have been the one to initiate things more. But because he was so sensitive, I didn't really know how to handle Russell. And when you don't know how to handle things you tend not to. So it was like we were mutually guarded around each other."

That was the great irony, of course. For in many of the important ways Cousy and Russell were very similar, both intensely driven, sensitive, private, both the architects of personal scripts no one ever could have envisioned when they were teenagers. They both were products of the generation that had shaped them, and they would carry that baggage with them their entire lives. They both had had difficult childhoods, Cousy as an only child in an immigrant home where affection seemed to be doled out sporadically; Russell with his mother's death when he was just twelve years old. Even in basketball terms, they both would be considered the ultimate overachievers in light of where they started from and the odds they had to surmount just to make their high school teams, let alone rise to the pinnacle of American sport. They both were great teammates, taking responsibility when they weren't playing well, totally committed to winning. Also, as they got older, both came to understand they were men still playing a child's game and that in a different world they should be doing something more socially productive. Russell once said he considered playing professional basketball "the most shallow thing in the world."

It would be easy to say it was race that complicated things, but that wouldn't be entirely accurate, because Cousy never had a problem with African-American teammates, either before Russell arrived or afterward. In fact, his two previous black Celtics teammates would later say how good he'd been with them, how sensitive he'd been to the adjustment of black players coming into the NBA. And there was no question that both Cousy and Russell immediately benefited as players from the other's presence, Russell's arrival instantly making the Celtics a great team, the kind of team Cousy had been searching for throughout his professional career. And because they played such different positions and were so different physically, the great big man and the great little man, it wasn't as though one's success diminished that of the other in any way. There was no question they respected each other both as players and teammates. So maybe it was something as easy to understand as Cousy's being seven years older and already the game's established superstar, whereas Russell was just a rookie, his professional career all ahead of him. Maybe it was the nature of professional sports, the nature of the workplace, where players left after practices and went back to their own worlds, their own thoughts and dreams going with them.

Whatever the reason, the Celtics' two overpowering superstars in the spring of '57 were mutually guarded with each other.

In the early years of the new millennium, while being interviewed for a television documentary on Russell, Cousy started crying on camera after being asked about the prejudice Russell suffered through as a player. He essentially said he should have been more sensitive to Russell's plight, saying he should have done more to help Russell at the time. Afterward, Russell told Cousy he shouldn't feel guilty, that there was really nothing he could have done to make Russell's stay in Boston any easier.

Or, as Heinsohn would later express in his famous statement: "No one understood Russell, not even himself."

Yet there's no question Russell had immediately changed both the Celtics and the NBA. No one had ever seen a player his size with the kind of athleticism he possessed, and from the beginning, that had made an impact on the game. His shot-blocking ability, his defensive intimidation—these were sneak previews of what the NBA would soon evolve into. Looking at Russell was like looking at basketball's future, while looking at the Hawks, as great as they were, was like looking at basketball's past.

The two teams' respective styles of play were different, too. The Hawks were representative of basketball in the fifties, a team that looked to pound the ball inside to their big people. It was traditional basketball, the way the NBA game had been played since the league had begun back in 1946, a half-court game dominated by big, relatively immobile post players.

The Celtics were the opposite, fueled by Cousy's ability to run a fast break and by Auerbach's commitment to a fast-paced style. The Celtics always were trying to push a game's tempo, speed it up—the style basketball would evolve into. Russell enabled them to be more effective doing that, for he could rebound and throw quick outlet passes to Cousy that started the Celtics' fast break. Then, on the other end of the floor, his athleticism and ability to block shots put tremendous pressure on the Hawks' inside men, however big and skilled they were.

Or, as the Hawks' six-foot-eleven center, Charlie Share, would later say, "The first time I ever played against Russell I knew the game was changing around me."

Years later, the seventh game between the Celtics and the Hawks would be remembered as one of the seminal games in NBA history, the game that did more to help the NBA in those years than any other. Some, Heinsohn included, still consider it the greatest seventh game in NBA history, even after all these years. If nothing else, it was the first game seven of the finals to be nationally televised, a visible message that this was, indeed a major league, worthy of the attention of the American public, no insignificant thing in a league that, in many ways, was still considered little more than filler between football and baseball.

It was a game between two of the country's great sports cities, Boston and St. Louis, two cities that had played in the World Series nine years earlier. There was no overestimating this on that April morning in 1957—not where a fledgling league, only eleven years old, was concerned, in a sport that was still trying to escape from its dance hall past and from the perception that professional basketball was played by goons in short pants. Basketball was still seen as a sport on the far side of glamour, little more than a barn-storming league where teams came and went like shadows in the night. There was no overestimating to be done pertaining to a league that didn't go west of the Mississippi River, or south of St. Louis. The last thing the NBA needed was another final series featuring the Fort Wayne Pistons, such as the one the year before, one that had all but screamed out minor league, which was exactly how too much of the public saw it.

And all the pressure was on the Celtics.

Hadn't one Boston sportswriter called them the best team in basketball history?

Weren't they supposed to have cruised through the Hawks on the way to their coronation?

But all that had changed in the first game of the series.

The Celtics had eliminated the Syracuse Nationals in three straight games to get to the finals, and that had been symbolic in its own right. Syracuse had been the Celtics' Waterloo, ending their season in the play-offs the past three seasons, complete with the bad blood that came with it, as Syracuse was a team known for liking to fight. It was a veteran team that revolved around its star, Dolph Schayes, one of the league's superstars then, a six-foot-eight forward from New York City who once had starred at New York University. He was big and he could shoot the ball from far out, two-hand sets with a high arc. They were led emotionally by Paul Seymour, a twenty-eight-year-old player-coach, who had no use for Auerbach. Nor did the Celtics enjoy playing in Syracuse, which was universally recognized as the toughest place to play in the NBA, courtesy of frenzied fans who jammed the On-ondaga War Memorial arena, heckled the players, threw things at them, tried to dump sodas on them, constantly screamed at Auerbach, and intimidated the referees. It had become so institution-alized that the unofficial word among referees was that with ten seconds left in the game in Syracuse, it was better just to run for the locker room. Back in the early days of the league, one ref had simply gone into the locker room at halftime, changed into his clothes, and left.

Shortly before the regular season had ended, Seymour had appeared at the weekly basketball luncheon at the Hotel Lenox in Boston's Copley Square after Syracuse had played in the Boston Garden the day before. He quickly went after Auerbach and the Celtics for what he considered their rough play.

"I didn't realize what had been going on with the Celtics yes-terday," Seymour said. "Schayes' mouth was battered and he took quite a beating. Judging from what I heard from Dolph, the Celt-ics were out to get Dolph, just as they did three years ago in the play-offs. Jack Nichols and Jim Loscutoff were the men who did it to Schayes. Something's got to be done to stop it. After all, Bob Pettit was hurt by Loscutoff this year, wasn't he? I don't think the players do it without orders. Maybe one of us coaches should take a poke at Red Auerbach and end all the nonsense."

Earlier in the year Seymour had said, "The Celtics will find a way to lose the play-offs. Someone in their ranks will do it. Auer-bach always has found a way to get the club licked."

It was a theme Schayes also had echoed prior to the series, telling those at the Boston basketball luncheon, "Don't worry, we'll make the play-offs and then beat the Celtics like we always do."

That had been the backstory of the series, the enmity that had existed between the two teams for years, especially toward Auer-bach. In one of the games, Seymour had been at the scorer's table over some hassle, and found himself standing next to NBA commissioner Maurice Podoloff, a diminutive man who was called "Poodles" behind his back. The Celtics were convinced Podoloff always had it out for Auerbach, and for Cousy, too, since Cousy had been one of the driving forces behind the birth of the National Basketball Players Association just a few years before.

"I'd like to punch Auerbach," Seymour said.

"To tell you the truth, Paul, so would I," said Podoloff.

But the Celtics had proved Seymour wrong, beating the Nationals in three straight games, payback for the past.

And now on this April morning, they were only one win away from their first NBA title, so close they could almost reach out and touch the trophy.

Hadn't the champagne been in their locker room in St. Louis two nights earlier before game six in St. Louis, just waiting for the celebration, until the score had been tied with just twelve seconds remaining? Hadn't they been all set to win until Hawks star Bob Pettit, with the clock winding down, had taken an off-balance shot that rookie Cliff Hagan had tipped in at the buzzer to win the game and tie the series at three games apiece, sending it back to Boston?

"They couldn't win this one which meant so much to them," St. Louis coach Alex Hannum said afterward, "and I'll wager we'll get them in Boston. We can always rise to the peak for one game."

Hannum already had made his presence felt in this series, even if he was to have a bigger one before this day was over.

That had happened before games three and four, both of which were played in St. Louis.

"They're a bunch of butchers, so taught by Red Auerbach," he said, singling out Celtics Jim Loscutoff, Cousy, Sharman, and reserve Dick Hemric for their roughhouse play.

"That's not true," Russell countered. "Red does not prescribe roughhouse basketball. I do not like to read or hear about that sort of thing. Hannum is trying to work in a psychological angle, hoping for sympathy from the officials."

The article had been written in the *Boston Herald* by Joe Looney, and he wasted no time giving his take on Hannum, who was near the end of his NBA career and essentially functioned as a player-coach for the Hawks, wearing a uniform, but rarely inserting himself into a game.

"Big Alec is actually the last person connected with the league who should comment on rough style of play," Looney wrote. "His fouling has been so flagrant over the years the officials don't even have to see the infraction, they can hear it because Alec is as subtle as a bulldog."

But the Celtics had now lost three games to a team that had been in last place in the Midwest Division at the All-Star break, and Brown had told his team they had better win it all, or there would be a shake-up, and it wouldn't be the coach who went. Brown already had spent too many years and too much money waiting for the Celtics to be fully embraced in Boston, and he knew they had to win for this to have a chance to happen; to lose would be a crushing defeat, not only for this team, but for the Celtics in Boston, this franchise that always had been fragile, both financially and figuratively in the hearts and minds of New Englanders. Making it worse for the Celtics was they had been beaten in that sixth game by a rookie who once had been their property.

"Nobody blocked Hagan out on the rebound after Pettit's shot," complained Frank Ramsey, who was on the bench at the time. "The last thing we said was to be sure and block everyone out, but Hagan wasn't blocked."

"I was trying to help Loscutoff cover Pettit," said Heinsohn, who had been matched up with Hagan. "Pettit got by Loscutoff and I ran over to help out."

"Loscutoff had Pettit covered," Ramsey insisted. "Hagan should have been blocked out."

It hadn't been the first time the Celtics were bickering among themselves.

It had started after the first game, one they had lost in double overtime in the Boston Garden.

"There were some hard looks and under-the-breath mutterings in the Celtic camp over the weekend while they were splitting the first two play-off games with the St. Louis Hawks," wrote Larry Claflin in the *Boston Evening American*, "and the team now realizes it will take more than a token effort to defeat the Hawks in this seven game series."

Claflin was one of a long stream of Irish-American sportswriters in Boston. Eventually, he would team up with the *Globe*'s Clif Keane to form one of Boston's first sports radio talk shows, called *Clif and Claf*. He was always opinionated and not afraid to take a stand, popularity be damned.

Claflin said that Heinsohn got some of the looks for his persistent outside shooting, even though he hadn't been shooting well from the outside, and that Russell got some for "taking the most important shot of the game when anyone but him should have taken it." He went on to say that Russell was not having the easy time of it that he had against Syracuse, when he averaged 28 rebounds in the three games, when he appeared at times to intimidate the Nats.

It all added to the theory that the Celtics had lost their swagger and were now feeling the pressure. They were complaining about the "whistle tooters," as the *Boston Herald* referred to the referees, specifically that the Hawks had been averaging six more free throw attempts a game. No one had expected the Hawks to be able to win this series, but here they were, still alive, and heading for a deciding seventh game. Adding to the drama was that Auerbach had complained after the sixth game in St. Louis that Hagan's winning basket in the sixth game had happened after time had run out.

So it's not surprising that when he saw referee Jim Duffy at the insurance counter inside the St. Louis airport the next morning, he ran up to him as if wanting to fight. Auerbach and the Celtics didn't like Duffy, anyway. They thought he was always sending the Hawks' star Bob Pettit to the foul line any time an opponent all but breathed on him, in addition to referring to him as "Mr. Bob." The night before, Duffy had been in charge of the game clock.

"Why didn't you have the clock stopped with three seconds to go when Bob Cousy called time-out?" yelled Auerbach.

"The game was over," Duffy replied.

"You've got no guts," he yelled at Duffy.

"Don't say that to me, you phony," Duffy shot back. "You've always been a phony."

Then again, Auerbach's getting in a referee's face was nothing new. It long had been part of his image, nose to nose with some ref, his ever-present game program rolled up in his left hand, spittle almost coming out of his mouth, arms gesturing, face flushed; he was the caricature of the crazed coach.

But this had seemed to have the potential to escalate into something nasty until Jocko Collins, the NBA's supervisor of officials, got between Auerbach and Duffy, separating them.

Eventually, Auerbach ran into Podoloff, who was also in the airport that morning.

"Who's refereeing tomorrow afternoon?" he demanded.

"I don't know," Podoloff said.

"They always seem to know in St. Louis," countered Auerbach.

"Here's where I came in," snapped Podoloff, hustling off to a gate and his plane to New York.

It was no secret the Celtics thought Podoloff and the NBA office wanted the Hawks to beat them. There had been an article in one of the Boston papers after the first two games saying how the Celtics knew the Hawks were the underdog, the more sympathetic team. It was one more reason they thought the refs were against them; one more example of the growing pressure they were feeling.

"We'll never win in St. Louis with that kind of officiating," owner Walter Brown said.

"I agree 100 percent," said Sharman. "This is supposed to be big league, but we get bush-league referees."

The sixth game had been the Hawks' third 2-point win in the series, and both Hagan and Pettit had been carried off the court in the jubilation that had been in Kiel Auditorium in St. Louis when the game ended. If there was anything to momentum, the Hawks certainly had it. They had begun this series as huge underdogs, and now they were just one game away from upsetting the vaunted Celtics and becoming the NBA champions. They now came into the Boston Garden on this Saturday afternoon riding on the back of momentum.

But from the opening night of the series, the Hawks had sent the Celtics a message all but outlined in flashing neon, much to the surprise of both the oddsmakers and the pundits.

It had been in the Boston Garden and the Celtics had been big favorites, even though the Hawks had come to town on a six-game winning streak in the play-offs. After the Syracuse win, many in Boston assumed the Hawks were no real match for the Celtics, to the point that only about half the thirteen-thousand-seat Garden was full. Not that this came as a real surprise, since the Celtics lagged far behind both the Red Sox and Bruins in popularity in Boston, and the game had been televised locally. Still, there was the feeling that the Celtics already had gotten by Syracuse, the real opponent, and this series with the Hawks was going to be easy in comparison.

Auerbach had been whistled for a technical foul two minutes into the game by referee Sid Borgia, with whom he always seemed to be feuding. Auerbach had been holding the ball. Borgia called for it. Auerbach rolled it to Cousy instead. That had done it. Borgia blew his whistle and slapped the technical on him.

It was an ominous beginning.

As was the Hawks' jumping off to a 13-point lead at the end of the first quarter. It took a tip-in by Heinsohn to get the game to overtime, but by then Russell had fouled out. A big shot by Cousy got the Celtics into the second overtime, but even that wasn't enough as the Hawks prevailed behind 37 points from Pettit. It was a winning basket the *Boston Herald* called a desperation heave.

"With 30 seconds to play in the second overtime period Jack Coleman, the St. Louis Hawks' statuesque forward, turned loose a sidearm scaler that nestled in the strings," the *Boston Herald* wrote.

It had been the first game in a while that Pettit had played without a cast on the left wrist he had broken in mid-February. He had been the league's top scorer before the injury. In the beginning, the cast had bothered him, but he played with it in the playoff victory over the Lakers, and had played well. Now the cast was off, and it was apparent the Celtics really had no one who matched up well against him. He was too big for Loscutoff, too good for Heinsohn, the rookie not known for his defense, and he was playing with the kind of confidence that comes from knowing he could put up big numbers against anyone in the league.

The next day the Boston newspapers criticized the Celtics for letting the game get away from them in the end, for losing their composure. The message was clear: This Celtics team, now in its first NBA Finals, was not supposed to lose to the Hawks.

It had been a great game, with two overtimes and the Hawks winning 125–123.

That first game had established the matchups: Cousy and Sharman guarded by Slater Martin and Jack McMahon; Heinsohn matched up against Ed Macauley; Loscutoff guarding Pettit, although Russell sometimes would take him; Ramsey usually guarding Hagan, who had been his teammate on great Kentucky college teams, and an old Kentucky high school rival.

Although the Celtics had come back in the second game to win by 20 in a sold-out Garden, the tone had been set. Nothing was going to come easy, no matter what the preseries scouting reports had said, or that the Celtics had won seven out of nine of the regular season games between the two teams. Cousy and Martin were going to go at it like cat and mouse, Martin hounding him all over the floor, making him work just to get the ball up the court, forever putting pressure on him, trying to wear him out. They had been playing against each other for seven years now, and they had deep mutual respect.

"He played me tougher than anyone in the league," Cousy would say years later. "He was as quick as I was, quick enough to get over the screen, and he could sustain it. He was a tough Texan, a tough, little guy."

They had had some words back and forth early in the second game, even if they ended up patting each other on the back and helping each other get up the rest of the game. It was one more example of the magnitude of the series, especially for Cousy.

"That's the first time Cousy and I ever had any trouble since we started playing against each other," Martin said afterward.

Even after that second game, the series tied at a game apiece, the Celtics were subdued in their locker room. They knew they had failed to hold serve in the first two games and now were going to have to win at least one game in St. Louis to win the series. Auerbach had little to say, and he even refused to go on a radio interview.

"We got what we wanted in Boston, one victory," the Hawks' Macauley said. "Now it's up to the Celtics to do the same thing in St. Louis. The pressure is on them now to win a game in St. Louis."

They had done that in the fourth game, the second game in Kiel Auditorium, a game where Cousy lost a tooth shortly after being hit in the mouth before the first half ended. Jack Nichols, a Celtic reserve who was also a full-time dental student at Tufts, came out on the court to attend to him. Then they came back to easily win the fifth game in Boston, a game in which Sharman had scored 32, and Cousy had dished out nineteen assists on a night when five thousand people had been turned away from the Garden for lack of room, something that never had happened before in Boston.

"What can I do to stop him?" the Hawks' McMahon had said of Sharman. "He's the greatest shooter in basketball. I'm not doing anything wrong, but there just isn't any way to stop him. The Celtics have set plays for Sharman now, and there's no way to get through the blocks they set up for him. Why, that Loscutoff is like a stone barricade for Sharman. He blocks me out and by the time I get through to Sharman, the ball is going through the strings. He never lets up for a second. Never mind about his shooting, how about his guts? He's a great competitor, as great as I've ever seen."

A column in the next day's *Boston Herald* by Larry Claflin said how Sharman had received a letter from his mother in California. She had been reading about the controversy in the series, especially Hannum's charges that the Celtics were "hatchet men." She had told her son to forget about them and to just keep on playing, even though the Sharmans and the Hannums were dear friends.

"Sharman didn't need his mother's advice," Claflin concluded, "because he never stops trying. The only way the Hawks can stop Sharman is to put a bomb in his luggage today when the Celtics fly to St. Louis."

That had been the sentiment heading into the sixth game, heightened by Hagan's having been treated for "water on his knee" after the fifth game, and Martin's having been seen limping afterward.

Regardless of the particulars, the series had proved to be a lot more difficult for the Celtics than anyone had thought. To make matters worse for the Celtics, Pettit always had great success against Russell, his ability to hit outside shots causing Russell to have to come out and play him, this negating Russell's obvious effectiveness around the basket. He also pounded the offensive glass, so even when Russell wasn't guarding him, he had to deal with Pettit when the Hawks missed shots. Russell had tremendous respect for Pettit, considering him to have the best second effort on the boards of any of the men he had played against.

"Pettit just hurts my pride," Russell told the Boston papers.

The Hawks had a huge front line, with both Pettit and Macauley at six foot eight, Charlie Share at six foot eleven, and six-foot-seven Jack Coleman off the bench. They were big and they were physical, a style that always had bothered the Celtics, who were considered more of a finesse team than a physical one; a team that wanted to get out and run, not engage in half-court, rough-and-tumble games. The Hawks also believed they could beat the Celtics, knowing that their record never had been a true barometer of their team, that there had been too much turmoil early in the season, plus an injury to Pettit in midseason. They knew they were now playing their best basketball of the season.

And now they needed only one more win.

But the Celtics had home court.

WILL IT BE CELEBRATION OR FRUSTRATION FOR BOSTON FANS? was the tagline in the *Boston Herald*, over a headline that screamed out CELTS IN TITLE SHOWDOWN.

That was the lead story in a sports section that also had Julius Boros leading the Greensboro Open, and the Yankees picked for first in the American League.

And for the first time in NBA history, a group of fans, rumored to be about twenty, had spent the night sleeping in the outer Garden lobby so they could be first in line for the public sale that was supposed to start at nine o'clock. Maybe this was the most remarkable thing of all for this franchise that had been financially shaky ever since its beginning just eleven years earlier; this franchise that never had been embraced in Boston, certainly not in those early years when one of the city's newspapers hadn't even covered their first game, considering a pro basketball team in Boston not as important as high school hockey.

And now they were going to play their biggest game in franchise history, a game that would have longtime repercussions and change the history of American sport.

Even if no one on this morning in April 1957 knew it.

CHAPTER TWO

On this morning you could buy a set of tires for $11 and a pair of Thom McAn shoes for $4.99, a new Dodge for $2,200, and a three-bedroom house in the suburbs for a little over $20,000. In the movies you could see *Oklahoma!* at the Saxon in downtown Boston, *12 Angry Men* with Henry Fonda at the Loew's State, *Heaven Knows, Mr. Allison*, with Robert Mitchum and Deborah Kerr, and *Lady Chatterley's Lover*, billed for adults only, at the Beacon Hill. You could also see *Fear Strikes Out*, the story of Red Sox outfielder Jimmy Piersall's emotional breakdown, featuring Anthony Perkins and Karl Malden as Piersall's father.

And on the front page of the *Boston Globe*, one dominated by a big, bold headline, NO MAIL DELIVERIES TODAY, courtesy of a postal strike, and a small story about the opening of the new Massachusetts Turnpike, was a small headline, CELTICS, HAWKS, CLASH HERE TODAY FOR TITLE.

The story was written by Jack Barry, one of the few Boston

sportswriters who liked basketball and always had championed the Celtics. He called the Celtics "the best team in basketball," and he wrote that "the game itself will bring to a rousing climax a struggle by both teams through 72 regular league games and nine post-season elimination contests. The championship squad will pick up $18,500 and the losers $17,500."

What it didn't say was how big the game was for the Celtics, specifically for Cousy and Auerbach.

They had been chasing the NBA title together for seven years now, through the bumps and grinds of too many NBA seasons, and never before had been this close. The year before, Cousy had been on the cover of *Sports Illustrated*, the slick new magazine from Time, Inc., then only in its second year. The article, written by Herbert Warren Wind, who would become a noted golf writer, featured six photographs of Cousy in his green road uniform, a feature that was called "Magician at Work." It said how he was twenty-seven, in his sixth season as a pro, and was being regarded as the greatest all-around player in the history of the game.

In many ways Cousy had become the face of the NBA, a name that everyone knew, even those who couldn't have named two other players in the league. Much of that was based on his style of play, his showmanship, even if no one called it that back then. Watching him play was like getting a glimpse of the game's future, how the game would evolve, although no one knew that either in the spring of '57. To see him play was like watching an artist staring at a blank canvas full of unlimited possibilities. There had been other great point guards in those early years of the fifties in the NBA, guys like Dick McGuire of the Knicks and Martin of the Lakers, even if no one ever called them point guards back then. They all could run a team, make the right pass, get the ball to the scorers underneath. They were the quarterbacks of their teams, especially McGuire, who later would be called "Dick the Knick," even though his basketball fame eventually would be eclipsed by his younger brother, Al, who would become one of the more colorful coaches in college basketball history. Cousy added another dimension, one that had been born in the school yards of his youth in Queens; with him it became a game that wore the imprint of the New York school yards, intuitive, improvisational, basketball as some form of creative statement, even if none of it was ever planned.

It's difficult to envision now, in this basketball world where self-expression is as omnipresent as slam dunks and expensive sneakers, but in the basketball world of the late forties, the world in which Cousy came of age, to stand out, to draw attention to yourself, to do anything against the norm, was considered almost sacrilegious. Nor was to do so in Cousy's personality. He was quiet, almost shy, never comfortable in crowds; one of the reasons he lived in Worcester throughout his career with the Celtics was that it gave him an excuse not to do a lot of public functions in Boston. One of basketball's little ironies is that he would be known for his flashy style, to the point that in the fifties and sixties, whenever some high school kid would throw some fancy, ill-timed pass, some coach invariably would say, "Who do you think you are, another Cousy?"

But it was never planned.

Instead, it evolved out of the way he'd come of age in the game, both in the school yards of his youth and in his college career at Holy Cross. It was there that several of the players used to fool around before practice with no-look passes, behind-the-back passes, things perceived as tricks back then, or else as the stuff of the Globetrotters, the extremely popular Negro barn-storming team regarded as showmen and entertainers, not serious players. These basketball tricks were never used in actual game practices, even though Holy Cross played a pass-and-cut style, the way the game was played in New York's school yards.

But Cousy loved this kind of stuff, for it came very naturally to him; with big hands and long arms, he was able to control a basketball in ways other six-foot-one players could not. He also had uncanny peripheral vision, enabling him to look down the court while also being able to see what was happening on both his left and his right. Fans were forever saying it was as if Cousy had eyes in the back of his head when he threw one of his famous seemingly no-look passes. Not exactly, but he did have a wider range of vision than most people, one of the special gifts he brought to the game. So there had been times when he would throw over-the-shoulder passes in games if he thought the situation warranted it. But it was not something he often did, which is why when he dribbled behind his back in a sold-out Boston Garden, Holy Cross against Loyola, a move that later would become his basketball signature, it seemingly had come out of nowhere.

"We were in a time-out," Cousy said. "We decided to hold the ball for one shot, and I was going to take the shot. After passing the ball around until the clock went down to about eight seconds, I started driving to the basket. I was on the left side of the court, going to my right. But when I got to the right side of the basket my opponent was on my right side and I had no room to shoot. I had no choice."

So without changing direction, he bounced the ball behind his back with his right hand, picked it up with his left, and then drove to the basket and made the winning shot with a sweeping left-handed hook shot. The Garden erupted in a hurricane of noise, people realizing they had just seen something they never had seen before.

Showtime had been born.

It would just take the Lakers forty years to market the phrase.

By 1950, Cousy had arguably become the most celebrated college player in the country, as much for his idiosyncratic style as anything else. Watching him was to watch something different even if you didn't always know what it was. One of his teammates was quoted as saying he was waiting for Cousy to make the basketball sing a song. Everywhere he went that winter he was the center of attention, as sportswriters crafted glowing tributes to his unique style. He also was praised by virtually all of the big-name coaches of the era, all of whom knew they were watching a kid with a special gift, even if it sometimes transcended the borders of what textbook basketball was supposed to be at the time.

"He is a basketball quarterback," said famed Kentucky coach Adolph Rupp, "and he will go down in history as one of the greatest basketball players of all time."

Those were prophetic words in 1950.

Cousy was now making about $22,000 a year, the highest contract in the league, but he had never won a title.

"I don't think the rest of us realized then how big the game was to Cousy and Sharman," Heinsohn would later say. "They had been chasing it for so long."

In many ways, though, the game was bigger for Auerbach.

We now view him as one of the all-time greatest basketball coaches, his nine NBA titles a testimony to that, his slice of basketball immortality assured a long time ago. That wasn't the case in 1957, however. He was not considered either a basketball genius or a visionary. He certainly wasn't viewed as the best NBA coach, that accolade given either to Johnny Kundla, who had the Minneapolis Lakers in the late forties and early fifties, or to Joe Lapchick, the highly respected coach of the Knicks, whose basketball roots went back to the Original Celtics in New York City in the early years of professional basketball. Auerbach wasn't even appreciated in the Boston Garden, where he was rarely cheered, never mind loved.

Instead, Auerbach was considered brash and arrogant, certainly a polarizing figure. He feuded with both referees and several fellow coaches. He also had a contentious relationship with many of the Boston sportswriters, who considered him both condescending and difficult, not to mention someone who seemed to lack many of the discernible social graces. In basketball terms, he often was considered a run-of-the-mill coach, just another guy on the bench in a suit yelling at referees, even though Walter Brown, his boss, was always defending him to the Boston sportswriters, forever telling them that he could outthink any coach in the league.

Years later, Bob Brannum, who had played for Auerbach and the Celtics in the early fifties, remembered the first time he had met Auerbach:

It happened in 1949, 1950. I was playing for the Sheboygan Redskins and Red was coaching at Tri-Cities. It was the year the National League was merged into the Basketball Association of America and became the NBA. There was a rivalry between Sheboygan and Tri-Cities you just wouldn't believe. And in those days in the NBA you won on your home court. Red used to get thrown out of the games a lot, and he'd go up in the balcony and coach from there. The fans loved to yell and scream at him. There was an old man, maybe 60 years old, and he hated Red, hated him. One night, Red went racing down the court on a bad call, and this little old bald-headed man runs up to him and belts him with a program, right on top of the head. Red turns around and starts hitting him, and I grabbed Red and held him off.

But if he already had come a long way from the tank towns of his early years in professional basketball, this game was huge for Auerbach in ways even he couldn't imagine.

If nothing else, it would be his validation.

He already had come a long way from the Brooklyn of his childhood, coming of age in the Williamsburg ghetto in the twenties and thirties, the son of a man who had come from Minsk in Russia and ran a dry cleaning business. Williamsburg was an ethnic stew back then, and Auerbach spent much of his childhood helping out his father in a dry cleaning shop where they got $.15 for a shirt, or hopping onto the dashboards of taxicabs parked at red lights and trying to wash their windows for a nickel. It was there he learned the value of work, and it was in the street that he learned the value of survival skills: how to win an argument, how to get your way, how to impose your will in an insular Darwinian world where the pie was too small for everyone to get his fair piece. Maybe most of all, he learned early that no one is ever going to give you anything; if you want something, you have to take it. These were the twin tenants of his faith, the lessons from the street he always carried with him, no matter where basketball would take him. They made him a high school basketball star, second team All-Brooklyn in the mid-thirties, even though he was only five foot nine, and the schoolboy basketball world of his childhood was extremely competitive. Too many kids were trying out for too few teams, and basketball was already the city game in New York City.

Basketball got him to a place called Seth Low, a junior college affiliated with Columbia at the time. That led to a scholarship to George Washington, a long way from his Brooklyn childhood. There he fell under the tutelage of a man named Bill Reinhart who believed in fast break basketball. It was a new style, developed by a man named Frank Keaney at tiny Rhode Island State in the early thirties, that was based on the simple premise that the team that took the most shots at the basket often won the game. This was the style Auerbach later would bring to professional basketball. He had been one of those tough, feisty, backcourt players in college who got by on smarts and guile, not on great ability. These two traits would serve him well when he got into the rough-and-tumble world of professional basketball. Not that he ever set out to do so. He set out to go into teaching, a much more stable profession when he graduated in 1939. He soon landed a job at St. Alban's, a tony prep school in Washington, where he taught while working toward his master's degree.

But real life got in the way.

Specifically, World War II, which for the United States began in December '41, after he was already married and already had his teaching job. He ended up being stationed in Norfolk, Virginia, where he ran an intramural program on the base and coached a team that included Red Holzman, who would achieve his own sliver of basketball fame in the early seventies as the coach of the

Knicks. When the war ended, Auerbach returned to Washington and got involved organizing some Washington Redskins football players into an off-season unofficial basketball team. As fate would have it, that got him introduced to Mike Uline, who had made a fortune in ice-making machines. He also owned an arena in Washington. When Uline started the Washington Capitols in 1946 in the new fledgling basketball league called the Basketball Association of America, Auerbach convinced Uline that he could acquire players through his service contacts and that he should be the coach. His theory, as he explained it to Uline, was that since basketball was a regional game, the different regions played different styles, but that he would be able to attract players who played different styles, and his team would be better off for it. Or something like that, despite his never having coached a real team. No matter that many of the teams in this new league were hiring coaches who already had made a name for themselves coaching college teams. Not knowing anything about basketball, and no doubt impressed with Auerbach's ability to sell both himself and his vision of the future, Uline made Auerbach his coach.

He was twenty-nine.

"Here I was going up against great, great college coaches with big reputations, people like Joe Lapchick," he said, "and I was a complete nobody. I knew, consciously or subconsciously, the referees were going to listen when a guy like Lapchick objected to a call. When he had a beef, they were going to listen. But if I objected to something, they'd be thinking, Who's this punk kid? I was very much aware of this, and I knew I had to figure out a way to counteract it. So I became a fighting kind of coach. On and off the court, I was going to back my ball club right down to the wire.

"Right from the start, I was determined that if I was going be fired or be unsuccessful, it was going to be because I lacked the knowledge or I lacked the ability. It was not going to be because of some temperamental goddamn athlete who wouldn't do what he was told, or who wanted to take over my ball club. There was no damned way I was going to let that happen."

So a style was born.

He had a wife, he had a young child, and he was a professional basketball coach. It was not exactly the most stable of professions in the late forties and certainly not one with any stature or job security. Many professional coaches then tended either to be ex–college coaches or guys who essentially were self-taught, devoid of any real credentials, guys who often seemed to come and go with the seasons. Some were even player-coaches, guys who simply called time-outs when things were going bad, and substituted guys off the bench to give the regulars a rest. No one considered coaches all that important in the big scheme of things, not in professional basketball, which always was regional in the best of times, and chaotic in the worst, with teams forever coming and going, sometimes in the dark of night.

But the war was over, and the country was optimistic, full of big dreams. Sports were growing, including professional basketball, essentially propelled by arena owners who wanted something to put in their buildings on all those cold winter nights. They saw the success of college basketball in New York City, where large crowds were flocking to see showcase doubleheaders in Madison Square Garden. Unlike today's owners of professional teams, the men who owned professional teams then were not titans of industry. They were not considered wealthy. They were not gentlemen sportsmen, owning teams as a sort of plaything, as was often the case in Major League Baseball. They were men trying to hustle in postwar America, men with big buildings looking for anything that was going to draw people and get them to buy tickets, men who called themselves promoters. Mike Uline in Washington was one. Danny Biasone in Syracuse and Eddie Gottlieb in Philadelphia were two others. Walter Brown in Boston was another. No one was in professional basketball thinking they were going to get rich, not in a business with no security and no assurance it was even going to exist a few years down the road, never mind flourish. They were all just trying to survive.

"It was a tremendous decision at the time," Auerbach later said, "because I was giving up all my teacher security, and I used to think of myself as a teacher. But I had a master's degree and I figured I could go back to teaching if it failed. And I believed that if people would pay to watch college basketball, they would pay to watch the cream of the crop. So I took a shot."

Three years later, Auerbach left the Washington Capitols to go work for Ben Kerner, who owned something called the Tri-Cities Blackhawks and offered him a better deal. Kerner had moved the franchise from his native Buffalo after just nine games. It was a franchise drawing from the Illinois cities of Rock Island and Moline, and Davenport, Iowa, one more example of what a fly-by-night operation professional basketball was. Kerner was another promoter by trade, someone who had made his money printing game programs, now trying to carve out a business in this new basketball league that offered no guarantees. Auerbach said he wanted full control. Kerner agreed. So Auerbach left his wife and young daughter back home in Washington and set out for these small cities in the Midwest that no one back east had ever heard of. He was there for two years before Kerner meddled in a personnel decision Auerbach thought was his. He quit on the spot.

In a curious twist of fate, Kerner now owned the St. Louis Hawks, the team the Celtics had to beat on this Saturday afternoon to win their first NBA title, as the old Tri-Cities team had morphed into the St. Louis Hawks, after four years in Milwaukee. Kerner also already had had a very public confrontation with Auerbach, one more chapter in their blood feud that had started back in the Tri-Cities.

Kerner, called "Benny the Boob" behind his back, was both colorful and combustible, much like Auerbach, constantly feuding with just about everyone. One of the more bizarre episodes had occurred three years earlier with the Celtics, and hadn't even involved Auerbach. Instead, it had between Kerner and Johnny Most, the Celtics' young broadcaster. From Brooklyn, Most had once had been on the football team at the University of Alabama, a time in his life of which he once said, "I was a spectator with a number on my back." He then had transferred to Brooklyn College, where he was a linebacker on a team quarterbacked by Allie Sherman, who later would go on to coach the New York Giants.

Most had been an aerial gunner during World War II, flying twenty-eight combat missions and earning seven medals. He had become the Celtics' broadcaster in 1953, replacing Curt Gowdy, whose real job was as the Red Sox' broadcaster. Most, as New York as an egg cream, would go on to be the radio voice of the Celtics for roughly forty years, although no one knew that then. All anyone knew then was that Most was a certified character.

"I wasn't born," Most once said. "Damon Runyon created me."

Most had been Marty Glickman's sidekick on New York Giant's football games in New York before he came to Boston.

Auerbach had been looking for a broadcaster to sell the team, someone to pump the product, and he didn't have to tell Most twice. He had a raspy, distinctive voice that sounded like sandpaper coming through a microphone, and from the beginning he viewed a Celtics game as a modern-day morality play, a battle between good and evil in sneakers, seeing the world through a green lens. There was no gray in Johnny Most's world. From his first broadcast no Celtic even committed a foul, and the referees were all part of some secret cabal conspiring to steal from the Celtics what was rightfully theirs. He called Cousy "Rapid Robert," Russell "Big Bill," Loscutoff "Jungle Jim," and he seemed to have a nickname for everyone. To Most, professional basketball was all wonderful theater, complete with villains and referees who always were conspiring against the Celtics.

He always opened his broadcasts saying, "Hi there, this is Johnny Most, high above courtside," words that eventually became as much a part of the Celtics as Red's cigars and the Boston Garden's distinctive parquet floor. "High above courtside," where the Celtics were getting ready to do "basketball battle," he would be the play-by-play man until 1990, an NBA institution, but even by '57 he was at the top of his game, the very definition of a radio "homer," and exactly what Auerbach had wanted.

Before a game one time in St. Louis, as Most was getting ready to go on the air, Kerner walked by him and said, "You're broadcasting for a bunch of assholes, starting with Auerbach."

Most quickly dropped his earphones and punched Kerner in the face. The two began throwing roundhouse punches at each other, both ending up on the floor.

That had been just the prelim, however, to Kerner's fisticuffs with the Celtics.

The third game of these NBA Finals had been in Kiel Auditorium in St. Louis, a cavernous building that seated about ten thousand and had been built as a theater, to the point that a curtain divided the basketball arena from the auditorium.

"Going to a Hawks' game was like going to the theater," said Greg Marecek, who would grow up to be a St. Louis media icon. "You entered the building walking up a tunnel. It was dark and dingy and then you eventually got to the concourse where the court was and there were lights over the court. It was an incredible effect. Those lights seemed like candles and they were the only light, except way up in the ceiling there were other lights that were softer, like a soft glow, so that all the attention was on the court. And the lights were so bright that the Celtics' green road uniforms used to almost glisten, while the Hawks' home uniforms were pure white. It was a wonderful place to watch a game."

Underneath one of the baskets was a stage, and below the stage was an orchestra pit. Kerner was forever having entertainment along with a Hawks' game, to the point that when the game ended and the people would file out, the orchestra pit would rise and there might be a concert by someone such as Guy Lombardo or Glenn Miller, all part of Kerner's grand plan to get people to keep coming to Kiel. One year he had clown Emmett Kelly perform for kids after every Sunday afternoon game, and one time Heinsohn came out of the dressing room and famed comedian Jack Benny was standing next to him. It was not uncommon for the game program to have an entertainer on the cover. Kerner always knew it was more than basketball.

There was a sense of glamour about a big game in Kiel, which had been built in 1934, the sense that it was more than just a basketball game, it also was a night out on the town, where it was not uncommon on a Saturday night to see women in mink coats and men in suits in the good seats. It also was not uncommon to see members of a Dixieland band moving through the crowd. In that sense, it spoke to what the NBA would one day become, not like the Boston Garden, which spoke to what the NBA was, even if the all-white Hawks team on the court in many ways symbolized the NBA of the era.

The Celtics dressed in a room that had mirrors with little lights over them, a room that was upstairs from the basketball court, what Cousy called "a little Mickey Mouse room." Then they had to walk down through the crowd behind one of the baskets to the floor, all the while being yelled at and heckled.

This was common throughout the NBA then. In a sense, professional basketball was similar to professional wrestling—full of outrageous fans who thought nothing of throwing things at players, screaming at them, even hitting them if they got the chance. Fans loved fights, many bringing a bloodlust through the turnstiles as well as their tickets. Pro basketball was a rough-and-tumble game.

But it was one thing to heckle and yell at players, something that seemed as much about the sport as knowing you were never going to get a big call on the road.

It was another to yell racial epithets, which came with the territory when Russell played in Kiel. Slurs were routinely called out to him, from "nigger" to "coon," to "Go back to Africa, you baboon," to "black nigger," to any other racial epithet people could come up with in a city that was still segregated.

"Watch out, Pettit—you'll get covered in chocolate," a fan once yelled out.

Russell once called St. Louis "the loneliest town in the world."

Certainly it was a place where he wasn't allowed in the down-town restaurants, not even in the greasy spoon where the rest of the players went to eat late at night. His presence on the team also decided where the Celtics stayed in St. Louis, a place called the Hotel Melbourne, one of the few downtown hotels that allowed black guests.

Even by his first year in the league Russell had to battle the loneliness on the road, the little hotel rooms that often seemed to close in on him. There were too many hours, too much time when it was just him, alone with his thoughts, wondering what he had gotten himself into. Not that anyone ever really knew the depths of his periodic misery. To the rest of the world he would hide behind his stoic demeanor, his public face, the one that masked how essentially alone he felt.

This, too, was part of Russell's journey through the NBA in his first year, this feeling that in many of the important ways he was alone. In the years that would follow, he would have some black teammates, but not then, not in '57. He also was a loner by nature, the most private of men even to the people who knew him best. There was a remoteness about him, an unpredictability, the sense that one minute he could be joking and laughing, and the next off in some private world to which only he had the password. No one had ever come into the NBA with the baggage he had. No one had ever experienced the racial hatred he heard from some fans.

And St. Louis was the worst city he visited.

Players were forever complaining about being stuck with hat pins on their way through the stands from the dressing room to the court.

"They gave them fits," Pettit said about the Kiel Auditorium crowd. "They were as great a group of fans as I saw anywhere. Just sensational. They were loyal and a great help to us."

It also was a crowd that hated the Celtics, especially Auerbach, who was forever yelling at the officials, stirring everything up. They might have appreciated Cousy's wizardry, but without a doubt, the very sight of the Celtics coming down through the crowd to get to the polished court raised the energy level of everyone in the building—especially after the Celtics had gotten Russell, the rights to whom Kerner had traded away.

It was the first game of the series to be played in St. Louis, the series tied at a game apiece. Minutes before it was to start before a sellout crowd, both Cousy and Sharman had complained to Auerbach that one of the baskets was a shade too low. So referees Sid Borgia and Arnie Heft had a maintenance man begin to check the rims. Auerbach fumed, thinking this was just one more cheap trick by Kerner and the Hawks, like their other stunts of always seeming to give the Celtics old basketballs to warm up with and always trying to do something to upset him—anything to get an edge.

"Auerbach, you're bush," yelled Kerner from about ten feet away.

Auerbach walked over and landed a wild right hook to Kerner's mouth.

Kerner responded with a slap.

"Not only are you bush, but you can't throw a punch, either," he yelled back at Auerbach.

Auerbach walked away, his back now facing Kerner.

"Ben," he said, "why don't you go find some ice to put on that fat lip I just gave you."

But he wasn't finished, not quite.

"Hey, Red," Borgia said. "How can a heavyweight like you allow a middleweight like Ben to land a punch? You're as bad a boxer as you are a coach."

"Well, I'm not the guy who has to get first aid," Auerbach countered. "I could have knocked him out, except the son of a bitch would have sued me."

Someone came out and gave Kerner a handkerchief for his bloody mouth. Then someone else came out to mop the smatterings of blood from the court, while Auerbach came back to the bench, fuming and rubbing his knuckles.

"Now you know how I feel in St. Louis, Red," whispered Russell.

All this transpired with the NBA commissioner sitting at half-court and with ten thousand fans in the building.

Was it the legacy of Auerbach and Kerner's time together in the Tri-Cities, or was Auerbach just aggressive and combative in the heat of the moment?

"He cussed me out," Auerbach told the press afterward. "What he called me was unprintable. I wasn't going to take that."

This was vintage Auerbach, especially in those early years before he won and the perception of him changed. This was the Williamsburg of his youth coming through; this was the Auerbach who was going to take shit from no one, the Auberbach who had come out of the ghetto of his childhood believing that in the end, it was either you or the other guy. This was the Auerbach of legend in those early years, the one who used to yell at both fans and referees alike, the one who was going to win or die trying.

It also happened in a certain time and place, the NBA of the fifties, a time when fighting in professional basketball was much more common than it is in today's NBA. And because it was more common then, it had few ramifications. The fight ended. The game started. Auerbach coached. Life went on.

"Aw, all I called him was a busher," Kerner said later. "He's a big sorehead. That stuff he was pulling was bush. With all the talent, he still has to pull tricks like that."

If nothing else, the incident only raised the ill feeling building between the two teams, resurrecting Hannum's quote that the Celtics were "hatchet men," and Brown's comeback that Hannum always had been a butcher and was lucky to be in the league.

"That man does everything to provoke me every time he comes into my building," Kerner later said. "He wants to run the whole show. You'd think he was the home team. He yells at the scorer's table, runs up to the P.A. announcer, barks at the officials, incites the fans, stomps around—hey, anything's possible when Red comes to town."

Before the fifth game, Podoloff fined Auerbach $300 for "unbecoming conduct" for punching Kerner, which caused Russell to say, "I only got fined $25 for whacking Ray Felix."

"Yeah," Cousy quipped, "but Red has seniority on you."

The fine angered the Celtics, though, providing one more example that Podoloff didn't like them.

"I'm ashamed of Auerbach for throwing the punch," Brown said, "but I'm also ashamed of Kerner and of Maurice Podoloff for not fining Kerner as well as Auerbach. Throwing punches belongs in the Blackstone Valley League, not in the NBA, but from all I hear, Red had some provocation. If Kerner called Red what he said he did, I don't blame Red for punching him. It appears to me that Podoloff doesn't like either Auerbach or Cousy and takes it out on them every chance he gets."

Auerbach would later say, as a defense, that having once been

sucker-punched as a kid, he had vowed never again to let someone get the first punch in. What he didn't say was that it had become a metaphor for his life.

But it was no surprise Auerbach was on edge.

He had waited a long time to be in the NBA Finals, and there
must have been a lot of long, lonely nights along with those long
nighttime train rides and bumpy airplane rides when the Finals
seemed as far away as the dark side of the moon.

In the beginning, the NBA had been ruled by the Minneapolis
Lakers and their center at the time, George Mikan, the NBA's first
superstar. Slow and a bit clumsy, he was the kind of player who
seemed to belong in some old newsreel of the early fifties, with
his hook shots and his big glasses with metal rims, his body all but
rooted to the floor. In many ways, Mikan had been the personification of what many people didn't like about professional basketball back then; it seemed to be played by circus freaks. Mikan's
six-foot-ten stature was so extreme in the early fifties that he was
viewed as almost otherworldly. Mikan had gone to DePaul in Chicago, where he had played for Ray Meyer, who would become one
of the college game's legendary coaches. Mikan had started out at
Notre Dame, where his career hadn't worked out, but at DePaul,
he went through a rigorous conditioning program, complete with
hundreds of hook shots with both hands every day. By the time
he got to the Lakers in the late forties, he would get the ball in
the low post, just off a lane that was only six feet wide, and swing
his left arm out as if he were an offensive lineman keeping line-
backers away from the quarterback; no one could stop him. He was
so effective that he later would be called the best player in basketball's first half century, so big a star that the Madison Square Garden marquee would say KNICKS VERSUS GEORGE MIKAN. He had

been the horse the Lakers had ridden to three straight titles in the early fifties, back when it seemed as if no one was ever going to be able to beat Mikan and his Lakers.

It must have seemed to Auerbach then that he always was going to be a basketball Sisyphus, always running up the mountain and never being able to get to the top.

He had sacrificed a lot to be the coach of the Celtics, in the middle of this NBA life he had carved out for himself. His wife and two daughters lived in their home in Washington, DC. He lived in the Hotel Lenox in Copley Square in Boston, in a ninth-floor two-room suite that looked out on the Boston Public Library, sneaking back to Washington when he could. In many ways it was a lonely life, that loneliness captured in the image of his often bringing Chinese food back to his room, where he ate it alone, only to heat up the leftovers for breakfast the next morning. He had his team, but he wasn't particularly close with any of the players. Some NBA coaches of the time would go out drinking with the players after games. Auerbach never did. He was their coach, after all, not their friend. This was a distinction never forgotten, a line never crossed, for he intuitively knew that if he did cross it, he never again could be truly effective as a coach.

There were no assistant coaches to hang out with on the road, as there are today. There was no traveling secretary, no one to smooth the difficulties inherent in playing on the road. There was no general manager. There was no assistant coach. In the early years, there hadn't even been a trainer. It was just him, alone in his hotel room eating his Chinese food, getting ready for the next game, always another game. This was his life, and in the manner of men who had come of age in the Depression, he took nothing for granted.

There is a picture of him coaching in the Boston Garden in 1957. A black-and-white photograph, it seems to be in shades of gray, almost as if it had been shot through smoke. There is a dingy quality to it, so clearly of a different era, many of the fans behind him wearing jackets and ties. Auerbach is standing up, yelling at someone. He is wearing a dark sport jacket and dark slacks. His hair is receding.

He was thirty-nine.

But here he was in his first NBA Finals, eleven years after he first began coaching in this league that had become the National Basketball Association of America. Here he was with what some writers were calling the greatest basketball team ever assembled. But now the series was tied at three games apiece, and the Hawks were owned by Kerner, as if there were a certain cheap symbolism in all this. To get what he wanted most in all the world, Auerbach was going to have to beat this man with whom he had such a history.

CHAPTER THREE

Boston was a very different city then from the one we've come to know. There was no Prudential building in Copley Square, no John Hancock building, the two buildings that have come to be synonymous with Boston's skyline for the past forty years. There was no Government Center, no City Hall Plaza. Instead, that area was called the West End, and it was dominated by Scollay Square, a warren of narrow streets with numerous sailor's bars, tattoo parlors, penny arcades, shooting galleries—a notoriously seedy section that already was an endangered species, targeted for a massive urban renewal project. It once had been called an area that "flows the deepest and most agitated currents of humanity."

Once, Scollay Square, so named for mid-nineteenth-century militia officer and real estate developer William Scollay, had been the home to the city's elite. Even before that, it had a rich history dating back to when the British troops had been housed there during the Revolutionary War. It was where many of the Irish settled when they first came to Boston, pushing the city's elite into nearby Beacon Hill and the Back Bay, and it became the commercial center of the city. It also had been one of the center-pieces for the 1919 Boston Police Strike when Governor Calvin Coolidge ordered the cavalry in to break up a mob demonstrating in Scollay Square.

By the early 1900s, the area had become a monument to vaude-ville and burlesque dancers, the centerpiece being the Old Howard Theater. Many of the biggest entertainers of the age came through Scollay Square, everyone from the Marx Brothers to George Burns, from Abbott and Costello to Milton Berle. The unofficial word was that you couldn't get a Harvard degree until you had frolicked in Scollay Square, especially with the strippers at the Old Howard. On the night World War II ended, Governor Maurice Tobin de-clared a two-day holiday, and one of the biggest parties in the city's history flooded into Scollay Square.

But by 1957, much of the party music was gone.

In a sense, it was symbolic.

Boston was a city having a difficult time coming out of the ef-fects of World War II, a city struggling with both the loss of the textile industry and the shipping industry, two longtime staples of its commerce. The Boston Navy Yard also had been cut back, one more sign of the city's troubles. Scollay Square was another. It had become a virtual monument to urban blight, the glamour gone, replaced by sailors and drunken college kids going to seedy strip clubs and eating late-night hot dogs at Joe & Nemo's. Like Scollay Square, much of Boston seemed mired in the past tense.

"Boston went down the tubes after World War II," said Scott McKay, a former *Providence Journal* reporter now writing a book about New England politics. "It deindustrialized. The shoe industry went bust. The textile industry went bust. They all moved out in search of cheaper labor. You had three generations of people living in public housing. And these were white people. There was very little opportunity. So everything became either a federal or a city job, and to get those, you had to know somebody. Politics was the way you moved up. Everything became political."

It also was a city locked in a seemingly age-old internecine struggle between the Irish politicians, who controlled the patronage jobs, and the Yankee financial establishment that controlled the wealth. This had been the split ever since the Irish, who had first started arriving in huge numbers after the potato famine in Ireland in the 1840s, had gained political power in the early years of the twentieth century.

Boston always had been a virtual blueprint for patronage as political clout, and maybe no one had symbolized it more than James Michael Curley, the old rascal king himself, who had first been elected mayor in 1914. The son of Irish immigrants, he had been elected mayor four times, and to Congress twice. Once, he was even elected while under indictment for mail fraud. He was everything the Yankee establishment didn't like: brash, flamboyant, powerful, Irish Catholic. He gave out jobs to cronies, played to class divisions, flaunted his ethnicity, and made Boston politics all about the Irish-Yankee war for control of the city, us against them. And when he was released from federal prison in Connecticut in 1948 by President Truman, he was met at the Back Bay train station by a band and legions of adoring fans who sang "Hail to the Chief."

He returned as mayor and quickly said, "I have accomplished more in one day than has been done in the five months of my absence."

He had been adored by the working-class Irish and despised by the Yankee elite, whom he contemptuously referred to as the "State Street Wrecking Crew." They, in turn, retaliated by taking some of their business out of the city and going off to Route 128, the new highway that ringed the city and later would become the center for Massachusett's high-tech boom in the 1980s.

But on this day in April '57, things were changing, too. Curley had been defeated in the '51 mayoral race by John Hynes, a man who once had worked for him and whom Curley derisively had referred to as a clerk. But Hynes had a very different style. He was less a caricature of the Irish politician of the times, making him better suited to try to get along with the Yankee establishment that always had controlled the wealth, those who had gone to Harvard and the best prep schools, those who belonged to the prestigious downtown eating clubs and summered on Cape Cod.

"He is a battle-scarred warhorse whose votes rest in the cemeteries of the long past," Hynes said of Curley.

So Curley, his time over, was jettisoned by a city that had been described in 1949 as having "a corrupt mayor, a corrupt city council, a swollen city payroll, and the highest taxes under the wandering moon."

The city was full of people of Irish heritage who had survived the war and wanted their little slice of the American Dream, too, one that included escaping the city and the tenement culture of the neighborhood, and getting that house in a suburb somewhere, and maybe a station wagon full of kids going off to Little League practice. You could go to college on the GI Bill and get a job better than your father had; you could be a part of a suburban world that seemed all about the future, not about having to carry a sign on election day and depend on some politician to get you a city job. In the fifties, Boston lost 13 percent of its population, many leaving the three-decker neighborhood for the suburbs.

So began the rise of the "two-toilet Irish," the tribal euphemism for the ones who had made it out of the city, the ones who had escaped to green grass and having a lawn of their own. The kind of Irish politician they identified with was John F. Kennedy, with his style, academic credentials, and his urbane polish, not some ward boss marching in some St. Paddy's Day parade in South Boston wearing a green hat and singing beery Irish songs. Kennedy was thirty-nine, now in his fifth year as one of the senators from Massachusetts, complete with a Harvard degree, a diplomat father, and presidential ambitions. In all the important ways, the Kennedys were philosophically different from Curley. They were a family that played to its Irish heritage on election day, but in terms of lifestyle and education, they long ago had moved out of the neighborhood, outdoing the Brahmins at their own game, complete with their own family compound in Hyannisport on Cape Cod.

Kennedy had begun thinking about running for president the year before after Adlai Stevenson had lost for the second time against Eisenhower, and in this year alone he had received more than twenty-five hundred speaking engagements across the country, all designed to raise his national profile. His opponents always were trying to dismiss him as a lightweight, but this was a new America, one in which every other day more people seemed to have television sets in their home, an America already hooked on popular culture, and Kennedy's looks and style made him a celebrity in ways that far transcended what his voting record was. That, too, hadn't been lost on Kennedy's father, Joseph, who aspired to nothing else than beginning his own political dynasty, one with goals far loftier than the office of the mayor of Boston, which his wife's father, John "Honey Fitz" Fitzgerald, had held in the early half of the century.

With the same pressure he would use to push all his sons into politics, he urged his son to make a run for the presidency, for he believed the country was changing.

He would tell the *New York Times* that America was no longer "a private preserve for Protestants," that there was a whole new generation out there filled with "the sons and daughters of immigrants who would be mighty proud that one of their own would be running for president."

One of the most popular novels of the year before had been *The Last Hurrah*, a fictional depiction of Curley at the end of the trail, an era ending with him. In 1958 it would be turned into a movie starring Spencer Tracy.

That, too, seemed symbolic.

An era was ending in Boston, and out of its ashes would emerge the "New Boston," a city far less parochial than what had preceded it, a city of vision poised for the future. Its symbolic centerpiece would be Government Plaza, the futuristic, soulless edifice built on the land that once had been Scollay Square and the West End. More than a thousand buildings were gutted and twenty thousand residents were displaced to clear the way for this construction. It was designed by renowned Chinese architect I. M. Pei, who seemingly cared little for Boston's past, and everything about its future.

Three years earlier, Hynes had said he wanted to form a coalition of government and business leaders, the first step in his plan for the city to revitalize itself, complete with removing the downtown slums and rebuilding the downtown business district. Included in this, his grand plan, was a new government center, a new World Trade Center, a second harbor tunnel leading out to Logan Airport, and a new highway system. But on this April day in 1957, that vision was still a few years away, maybe best captured by a *Boston Globe* photo of Mayor Hynes and some other civic leaders looking at a model of what one day would be the new Government Center.

Boston was a city in transition, just as the Celtics were in April '57.

No longer were they seen as a complete afterthought on the Boston sports scene, not now that they were in their first NBA Finals. They were now in front-page newspaper headlines, staring at an NBA title, full of big dreams. They, too, were looking at a bigger piece of the American Dream, just as were the "two-toilet Irish." They, too, believed in better futures.

And maybe no one symbolized this more than Cousy, who already had come so far from the emotional impoverishment of his youth, that little house in Queens where there had never been enough money or enough love. He believed in the same thing the "two-toilet Irish" believed in—this very American sense that it was possible to reinvent oneself, script one's future. A person's future did not have to be tied to his past.

In retrospect, this is not surprising. All around him was an America in the midst of tremendous change, a country rushing toward the future. The Korean War had ended four years earlier, and even if the threat of Communism had created the country's new fascination with fallout shelters, America was an optimistic place.

The Celtics were optimistic, too.

The Boston Garden was only about a jump shot away from Scollay Square, virtually on the border of the West End and the North End, the heavily Italian neighborhood full of narrow streets and restaurants and churches, an old ethnic world where many people were crammed into tenements. They showered in community bathhouses, and the elderly women dressed all in black. It was on Causeway Street, with its elevated train tracks and the clang of MBTA tracks a constant cacophony. Across the street from the green tracks was a scene out of an old late-night black-and-white television movie, classic film noir. A cafeteria; pawn shops; hot pretzel stands; shoeshine parlors; winos who seemed to have stepped out of an Edward Hopper painting; enough shot-and-beer bars to satisfy a boat full of sailors on shore leave; and Sullivan's Tap, which had a bar as long as a city block—it was the Boston the tourists never saw, a reminder of what so much of downtown Boston had become. Grim and dirty and a snapshot of the past, it was not the "New Boston" the city planners wanted it to become.

"There wasn't a whole lot of reason to go into Boston in those days," Cousy later said. "I went in for practice and games and then went back home to Worcester. I never felt I was missing anything."

The Garden was an old yellow-brick art deco building over North Station, where commuters ran every night at five o'clock to take trains to both the north and west of the city. There was nothing stylish about it. No luxury boxes, no suites, no club seating; it was just a big, cavernous auditorium with a lot of seats to fill. There was a hotel on one side called the Manger, and an office building on the other.

As John Powers of the *Boston Globe* once described it, "Walking along Causeway Street you belonged to another era, one that seemed perpetually stuck at nine o'clock in some bygone Friday night that smelled of cigar smoke and was fueled by Cadillacs and tweed overcoats, and men with flattened noses, ruined voices, and big rings."

The Garden had been the idea of Tex Rickard, a New York boxing promoter who had built Madison Square Garden in 1928, and whose dream was to replicate it in six other cities. The Boston Garden, originally intended to be called the Boston Madison Square Garden, had been built the following year, but Rickard died and the others were never built. The Bruins, who had been playing hockey in Boston since 1924 in the Boston Arena across the city, quickly moved in, and everything else was catch as catch can, everything from the circus to indoor softball, to midget auto races, to political speeches, to concerts. Walter Brown, who had inherited it from his father while still in his early thirties, did everything he could to fill the cavernous building. Franklin Roosevelt gave a speech there. Liberace once signed autographs until four in the morning after a concert. Notre Dame once even played a football game there. There were rodeos and softball games, dog shows and prizefights, and anything else Brown thought could entice people to buy tickets, his credo being that it wasn't important what he liked; it was important what the paying customers liked. But before the Celtics came in 1946, the only full-time tenants were the Bruins and a figure-skating exhibition called the Ice Capades, both of which Brown also owned.

On the first floor was a dark bar called the Iron Horse. Across the hallway were pinball machines and newspaper stands, and then the entrance to the main floor of the train station, where the ticket windows were, both for the various trains and for the Garden games, too. People always seemed to be coming and going, a bustle of activity. It was all frenetic. To get into the Garden itself, you had to walk up a succession of ramps, go inside, and there it was, more than thirteen thousand seats, the ones at half-court so close you could almost reach out and touch the players, complete with two balconies that seemed to hover over the court. But there also were seats on the sides behind poles, and always the seats were too small, as if built for a different era. Maybe most of all it looked quirky, everything sort of shoehorned in together, noises inside so loud that you couldn't hear yourself think in the big moments. It was a building that, even in the fifties, looked and felt old.

There were rumors that rats lived in the corners, and there was a famous story that a bunch of monkeys once escaped from the circus and were living in the rafters, coming down only when the crowds were gone to feast on the scraps left behind. Apocryphal or not, it all added to the Garden's mystique, the sense that the building was unique, a place full of old ghosts.

For this was a workingman's place. No pretense; no frills; no plush seats; no air-conditioning—it was a building as gritty as the neighborhood around it.

And hovering over everything was the smoke from a thousand Auerbach cigars.

That had become his signature, the victory cigar he would pull out of his coat and light up on the bench when he thought the game was over, much to the anger of opposing players and coaches, and to the consternation of his players. He wasn't the first NBA coach to smoke on the bench, that distinction supposedly going to Lapchick of the Knicks. But he was the first to smoke a cigar, and once he started doing it, he never stopped, lighting up whenever he felt the Celtics had the game in hand. It did not matter in the least to him that Hannum said one of his biggest wishes was to stuff the cigar down Auerbach's throat. It did not matter that Seymour of the Nationals once said he'd rather stuff Red's cigar down his smug throat than win an NBA title. It did not matter that the Celtics players all but cringed when they saw him do it, knowing how much it infuriated their opponents. It did not matter that everyone in the league thought it the very height of arrogance.

And it wasn't just puffing away on a cigar.

It was the way he did it, best described in the late seventies by Joe Fitzgerald, the longtime writer for the *Boston Herald*, who did Auerbach's autobiography with him: "Indeed, from the moment Red slipped his hand inside his sports jacket—quite often at the urging of a vulturous Boston Garden crowd—the entire production was as unpretentious as the closing death scene in *Macbeth*."

"That really started back in Washington," Freddie Scolari once said. "Talk about rubbing it in. He'd sit there with that big grin and he'd stretch his legs out in front of the bench. Then very slowly, he'd remove the cigar from his pocket, take off the cellophane and twirl it around, light up with a big flourish, then sit back and laugh. He never changed the act over the years."

The fact people didn't like it only made him do it more.

Or as Cousy once said, "Red was never one to pass on an opportunity to make it his trademark."

Frank Ramsey, the man Auerbach had turned into the best sixth man in the game, recounted the following exchange. "Red, it's not time yet. He'd say, 'We got this one.' I'd say, 'Red, not yet.' He'd light up. I'd say, 'What if we lose?' He'd say, 'We're not going to lose.'"

The locker rooms in the Garden were out of some lost era, a homage to every small-town midwestern gym in the middle of nowhere, for the simple reason that the Boston Bruins were the chief tenant in the building and got the best amenities, although in the Garden in the fifties, "best" was a relative term. The Celtics' locker room was a little room tucked underneath a stairway. One end of the room had a fifteen-foot ceiling. The other end was much lower. Each player had only one hook for his clothes, and Heinsohn said you knew you had made the Celtics when they gave you your own hook. There were two showers, and only one toilet, which was two steps up from the floor, and often water would flow onto the locker room floor.

It all seemed somewhat fitting.

So this was to be the biggest day in franchise history, the Celtics just one game away from their first NBA title.

Auerbach was not known for rah-rah speeches.

"There was none of that 'win one for the Gipper' stuff," Heinsohn said.

These were men with families, and they knew what the stakes were. The winning team was going to split roughly $18,000, so each player was going to get roughly $1,200. That was big money then in an era when almost all of them had off-season jobs, an era where no one believed professional basketball was ever going to be anything more than it now was, decent money for a nine-month job, but certainly not anything that was going to define the rest of your life, or even allow you to spend a lot of time in the off-season doing nothing.

They knew the Hawks.

The Hawks knew them.

But few of the players knew one another personally. Unlike

today, AAU culture and prestige summer camps, things that bring elite players together at a young age, did not exist. Colleges played mostly regional schedules. There were no games on national television, so few people were familiar with the best college players in the country, other than from stories in sports magazines. There was no ESPN, with its nightly *SportsCenter*, which has become the village square for sports in America. There was no sports talk radio. But with only eight teams in the entire NBA, the players came to know their opponents' games all too well, even if they rarely knew them personally.

Before games, Auerbach would pace around the room. Sharman would stretch and do exercises in front of his locker, the others looking at him as if he were crazy, for players rarely stretched before games or did any other kind of conditioning except to go through a layup line and take some practice shots. A couple, including Heinsohn, even smoked. Others might have been eating a quick pregame hamburger from some greasy spoon across the street. The room would be silent. Jack Nichols, a reserve forward, would tape anyone who needed it.

At some point Russell would go into the bathroom and throw up, something he did before most games, and certainly before big games, and to the others it was always a comforting sound, one that said the big guy was ready to go.

"Before the game Auerbach slowly picked St. Louis apart," Russell once wrote. "'Watch Martin do this. Watch Pettit do that. Remember that Macauley can't do this.' It was calm and rational in the dressing room. No hysterics."

CHAPTER FOUR

I t was a different sports world then in Boston.

The Red Sox were the undisputed kings, even if they hadn't won a pennant in a decade and were about to enter another season without a whole lot of expectation. They were led by Ted Williams, then thirty-eight, but still a towering presence in Boston. Teddy Ballgame could be many things—proud, imperial, arrogant, petulant, headstrong—but above all else, he was a superstar. From his movie star looks, to his infamous battles with sportswriters, to his having missed nearly five years in the prime of his career to fly airplanes in both World War II and Korea, to his living alone in the Hotel Somerset in Kenmore Square, he was larger than life. He had been playing in Boston since 1939, and to this day, a case can be made that he was the biggest star in the long history of Boston sports, still as charismatic a figure at the time of his death as he always had been. In 1957 he was like a god who periodically stepped down from Olympus to make a personal visit.

"Ted Williams would walk down any street in Boston and be mobbed," said Macauley, who had starred for the Celtics until being traded away in the spring of '56. "We all would walk down the street and nobody would notice."

All that, and sixteen years earlier Williams had been the last man to hit .400, finishing the 1941 season at .406.

So it was not surprising that the Red Sox dominated the sports pages in Boston, even though they had been mediocre the year before, Williams was in the twilight of his career, and they essentially were returning as the same team. Then again, the Red Sox always dominated the sports pages, year after year, regardless of their record.

Two years earlier had marked the death of one of the most popular athletes in the city's history. An estimated ten thousand people filed past his body at St. George's church in nearby Lynn when he unexpectedly died at twenty-six. His name was Harry Agganis, and he had been far more popular than anyone on the Celtics, with the exception of Cousy. The son of Greek immigrants, he became one of the most storied athletes in Massachusetts history. He was such a great high school quarterback at Lynn Classical High School that many of his high school games were moved to a nearby stadium in Lynn that could seat twenty thousand people. Notre Dame coach Frank Leahy called him the best high school football player he had ever seen.

Some seventy-five colleges courted him, but he stayed home to play at Boston University because he didn't want to leave his widowed mother. He made the undermanned Terriers at BU a big-time college football team. He was such a hometown hero that his freshman game against Holy Cross had drawn eighteen thousand people, and by the time he was a junior, he was one of the best quarterbacks in the country. In December 1952, when he was a junior, his BU team played Maryland in front of forty thousand people.

He was the first draft choice of the Cleveland Browns, but he signed with the Red Sox for a bonus of $50,000. Two years later he was in Fenway Park, hitting .251 with eight home runs in his rookie season. In one of those incredible scenes lending credence to the perception that he seemed to have stepped right out of the pages of fiction, on the afternoon he was scheduled to graduate from Boston University, he hit a home run in Fenway to win a game and then sped down Commonwealth Avenue in his 1953 Mercury just in time to attend his graduation ceremonies.

The next year he was hitting .313 in late May when he complained of not feeling well. A month later, while in the hospital, he died of a pulmonary embolism.

On the day Agganis died, the Red Sox were in Washington, about to play against the Senators. Both teams lined up on the baselines. Two Greek Orthodox priests conducted religious rites at home plate.

But Agganis was not the only local sports star back then, not in a city that loved its sports, a city whose rhythms often seemed tied to the changing of the sports seasons.

Harold Connolly, who had grown up in nearby Somerville, won the hammer throw at the '56 Olympics in Melbourne. Figure skater Tenley Albright from Newton won in the Winter Olympics that year in Italy. Prizefighter Tony DeMarco, Boston's own, was the welterweight champion of the world, often fighting in the Boston Garden.

In many ways, the fifties were a golden era of sports. The World Series was the biggest sports event in the country. It was played in the afternoons, and when the games were on either television or the radio, it was as if the country had taken a time-out. Attendance seemed to be up at everything from prizefights to auto races, from college basketball to the major golf tournaments. One of the fastest growing sports was the National Football League, which had started in the twenties as basically a mom-and-pop operation. Yet in the spring of '57, it was still a year and a half away from the play-off game between the New York Giants and the Baltimore Colts, the overtime win by the Colts that would become known as the one game that propelled the NFL into a major league.

Television, part of the new America, seemed to be growing exponentially as the decade progressed, creating new stars in the culture and in sports, too.

Amidst all this change, professional basketball was still fighting for respectability.

Until 1946 there was no NBA as we've come to know it. Before then, professional basketball in the East was little more than a succession of touring teams, such as the Original Celtics, based in New York City, one of its stars being Knick coach Lapchick. Some even played in steel cages to protect themselves from unruly fans. They often wore pads, and their games frequently resembled football scrimmages. They routinely were called "cagers," a name that stuck as the decades wore on, the favorite of newspaper headline writers.

The pro game had been around since the early years of the twentieth century, but there was no real money in it, certainly no glamour. Many teams played as warm-up acts in dance halls in the early years of the sport.

Something called the American Basketball League had begun

in 1925, but that had folded during the Depression. The other significant league was the National Basketball League, but "national" was a relative term. It was located in the Midwest, and companies sponsored its teams, the Cleveland Rosenblums, the Fort Wayne Zollner Pistons, the Indianapolis Kautskys, the Toledo Jim White Chevrolets. But with teams coming and going and players always jumping teams, there was little stability, so teams received regional attention at best.

So even by 1957, professional basketball was still a sport desperately trying to be taken seriously, not only by the sporting public, which tended to ignore it, but also by the big-name columnists of the big metropolitan dailies who had tremendous clout in shaping public opinion. Only eight years earlier there had been an article in *Sport* magazine titled "Basketball Is for Sissies." Its English author wrote that the game "is about as lively as a bit of conversation at teatime. Britain's male athletes would prefer to take on the hazards of a soccer match, and leave the refinements of the hoop game to the girls."

"We would sit around all those crummy locker rooms and complain about it," Cousy would say years later. "We knew we had a great game, the best game, but it was like nobody cared."

It was no secret that many of the country's top sportswriters, men such as Red Smith and Jimmy Cannon who worked in New York but were syndicated in many smaller papers around the country, had no use for basketball, never mind the new NBA. Their lives went from college football to spring training, with a few marquee prizefights thrown in. These were the sports with the mass appeal. All the others were more or less filler, save for the major golf tournaments. To them, basketball was decidedly minor league, especially in the aftermath of the college basketball point-shaving scandals of the early fifties that had been a body blow to the college game in New York.

The college game had been in New York since the thirties, represented by teams that generated a lot of interest but were hampered by small gyms and a lack of facilities that could accommodate that interest.

"This fool game is getting too big for its britches," said New York sportswriter Everett Morris one night when he and a few other sportswriters were trying to get into the tiny Manhattan College gym in Riverdale after the doors had been locked because the game was sold out. "Every gym in the city is hopelessly inadequate. Somebody should so something about it."

Somebody did.

A sportswriter named Ned Irish, who had ripped his coat that night while sneaking through a window to get into the game, became convinced the college game could be promoted and that people would pay to see it. His idea was to play doubleheaders, four teams instead of two, which would mean more fans, not to mention a better entertainment package for the customers. He put them in Madison Square Garden.

They were an immediate hit.

They created instant stars. They created intersectional rivalries. They created a new world of advertising and public relations for colleges, with proud alumni and enthusiastic students. And the Garden became the spiritual center of it, complete with its marquee that hovered over Eighth Avenue, with its glamour, its promise. The Garden became the place where every kid wanted to be, a place that whispered the bright lights and the promise of the Great White Way. These games even grew during World War II, although the war decimated the pro game, with bigger crowds and exploding interest, and college players who became national names. But then came the point-shaving scandals, followed by the countless stories and newspaper photos of shamed college kids trying to hide their faces. It was as though the college game were somehow tainted, at least in New York.

All the while the pro game was still largely perceived as a minor sport, a game beset by terrible officiating, coaches and referees constantly yelling at each other, a game with too many fouls and dominated by too many big men who were often viewed by the general public as freaks. The pro game was rarely seen as skilled, and often featured too many fights on the court and too few people in the stands. In their first few years, the Celtics were such a lousy draw in the Garden that when the Globetrotters were in town, the Celtics would play the early game and the Globetrotters the featured one.

It had only been eleven years since the NBA began, and even then it wasn't called the NBA. Not until 1949 would it become the National Basketball Association. In those beginning years, it was called the Basketball Association of America, with eleven teams in two divisions. The most northern team was the Toronto Huskies; the most southern teams were the Washington Capitols and the St. Louis Bombers. With the exception of the Providence Steamrollers, all the teams were in big cities, none west of the Mississippi River. It essentially was run by men who owned auditoriums and the hockey teams that played in them, so it was probably not surprising that the blueprint they were following was professional hockey and that the owners hired as their commissioner another hockey man, Podoloff, who was president of the American Hockey League.

To say it was ragtag is an understatement.

There was no 24-second clock. There were no jump shots. Very few players shot over 30 percent. Many teams used an old YMCA three-man weave, or else guards threw two-handed set shots from thirty-five feet. Centers often took sweeping hook shots from the foul line. The games were usually rough and slow. Bookies were known to move through the crowd, taking bets. The games themselves often were played in front of too few fans and in buildings that were too big. Referees often gave the stars every break, and the home team, too, the thinking being that if the home team won and the fans had a good time, they might come back. Bones McKinney, who had played in Washington for Auerbach and eventually would have a couple of footnotes in Celtics history, once shot two free throws with his back to the basket, complete with a big grin on his face.

This was the NBA's beginnings, the era that shaped Auerbach.

It was all about survival, both for franchises and players and coaches, too, a hard-edged Darwinian world of no guaranteed contracts, where players could virtually be cut on the spot. Or as Auerbach liked to remind his players, "I hired you, and I can fire you." Or better yet, "I may not always be right, but I'm never wrong."

Even in that first season, he made sure his players knew who the boss was.

This is what happened the time Auerbach challenged Freddie Scolari, one of his guards with the Washington Capitols. Scolari recalled the following exchange:

"'Hey, you little bastard, you think you're pretty good. But I could take you. You're not that good. I could take you.' The better night I had, the more he'd say it. 'Oh, those guys, they can't take you. But I'll take ya.' So one day I made him play me. I didn't want to hear any more. Do you know we played one-on-one and I shut him out? I was so mad at the guy that I murdered him. I wouldn't give him a chance to breathe. I think it was 24–0. But of course that didn't change his attitude. He was still the cocky little coach. That didn't bother him one minute."

There were too many nights when too few fans rattled around in big arenas, nights when you could all but hear the sneakers squeak on the floor, could hear the coaches yelling at the refs, the refs yelling back.

Was it any wonder games were often played in front of an indifferent public?

So there were ticket giveaways and promotions and cheap tickets and any other gimmick owners could think of to get people to see professional basketball. So the following year, zone defenses were outlawed, and in 1954, the 24-second clock was instituted. Both were changes designed to speed up the game and make it more attractive to people, as there once had been a game where Fort Wayne beat Mikan and the Lakers, the final score being 19–18. But it was never easy in those early years, to the point that in 1950 when Cousy was coming out of Holy Cross, he never viewed professional basketball as some promised land full of riches. He had never even seen the Celtics play during his four years at Holy Cross.

"I just wanted to earn a living and exploit my notoriety," he said. "I wasn't even thinking of the NBA, first because it seemed so Mickey Mouse, and no one from any team had ever spoken to me. I don't think I had ever seen a professional game."

Cousy and some of his teammates had organized a little barnstorming throughout Massachusetts and parts of New England against local town teams. It was called the "Bob Cousy All-Stars," and after the game, they would split the gate. It was a big success. Virtually everywhere they went, fans would pack the little gyms, and Cousy figured he would keep doing this until the people stopped coming. The key, he figured, was to try and find ways to keep his name in front of the public, whether it was playing in these little local All-Star games, or else starting a driving school and gas station with one of his college teammates.

He was getting out of college, he was planning to get married, and he knew he needed to find a way to make money, to be an adult. If that was to play for the Celtics, the hometown team, great. But it wasn't as if his childhood dream was to one day play professional basketball. It wasn't as if he had gone to college to prepare himself to play in this new league called the NBA. He just sort of assumed that if he was to play in the NBA, it would be for the Celtics. Not that he even knew when the NBA draft was. So when a sportswriter told him that he had been passed over by the Celtics and their new coach in favor of some six-foot-eleven center from Bowling Green, he was both hurt and surprised.

"Who picked me?" he asked the sportswriter.

"Tri-Cities," the sportswriter told him.

Tri-Cities?

Where was Tri-Cities?

Cousy quickly decided he wasn't going to go somewhere in the middle of Iowa to play professional basketball. He was making wedding plans, and he couldn't see himself dragging the both of them to Iowa. Tri-Cities. No way.

He eventually calmed down, and one day he flew to Buffalo to meet with Kerner, who despite owning Tri-Cities still had businesses in Buffalo. He told Kerner he wanted $10,000 a year; Kerner countered with $6,500. The meeting ended.

Kerner's next offer was $7,500. Cousy still said no. What he didn't know was that Kerner was trying to unload his rights to

Chicago. Then, before the season started, the Chicago Stags folded, the players being distributed to other teams. In the end, only three were left, Cousy among them. The other two were Max Zaslofsky, a proven star whom the Knicks coveted because he was Jewish and might be able to sell some tickets in New York, and Andy Phillip, a veteran guard. The three players were going to go to the Knicks, the Celtics, and the Philadelphia Warriors.

No one wanted Cousy.

After much haggling, it was decided the three names would be put into a hat. Celtics owner Walter Brown picked third; he got Cousy.

Cousy was getting his wish.

CHAPTER FIVE

From the Celtics' birth in 1946, it seemed as if the Celtics were always were running uphill on the Boston sports scene. As ingrained in the city as Boston Common and the swan boats in the Public Garden, the Red Sox had been playing since 1900. Even if they had not won a World Series since 1918, they had been to the World Series against the Cardinals in '46; they were the annual New England passion play, the region's hometown team. There was an affection for them, passed down from fathers to sons; politicians came and went, but the Red Sox were forever. The Bruins had been around since 1927, they had won the Stanley Cup in 1941, and Boston was known as a great hockey town.

It had never been a basketball town.

This was not without a certain irony.

For basketball was born only a couple of hours away, with James Naismith hanging up his peach baskets in the International YMCA Training School in Springfield, Massachusetts, in December 1891. Naismith, who was from northern Ontario, a bookish man with hair parted in the middle and wire rim glasses, was there to become a physical education teacher. One of his classmates was Amos Alonzo Stagg, who would go on to become the famed football coach. The two had even played together on a football team that had played against Harvard and Yale. Naismith was looking for something to keep his students busy in the long New England winter, the time Faulkner once called "the iron dark." After coming up with a few ideas for which his students had little use, he hung up the peach baskets and changed history.

For the game quickly caught on. Just two years later, Naismith brought it with him to Chicago. This was the same year as the first women's game, when the Smith sophomores played the Smith freshmen in Massachusetts. In 1896 Yale played Penn in the first intercollegiate game, and five years after that the first intercollegiate league was formed. As early as 1906 many of the New England colleges were playing it, and in those early years the heart of the game was in New England as it caught on in the high schools. Throughout the first half of the century, the game was growing exponentially, played everywhere—colleges, high schools, town teams, youth leagues, YMCAs.

So what had happened in Boston?

From 1925 until 1945 the sport hadn't even been played in the Boston public schools, so no generation of city kids had grown up with the game.

"Kids from Boston would go out to Great Lakes or somewhere like that for their military training in 1941, 1942, and 1943 and they wouldn't know what to do when someone brought out a basketball for recreation," Joe Looney, a longtime sportswriter for the *Boston Herald* once said. "While kids from Madison, Wisconsin, were throwing in hook shots, our guys would stand around scratching their heads."

But it was even more than that.

"Nobody even knew what basketball was about," said Howie McHugh, the Garden's public relations director. "We thought it was a sissy game, and I wanted no part of it."

Is it any wonder that for the most part the Boston sportswriters had either little interest in basketball or downright no use for it?

The team's name had come on a whim. Brown and McHugh were sitting around trying to come up with something—Unicorns, Whirlwinds, anything—until Brown essentially suggested, given the large number of Irish in Boston, why not call the team the Celtics?

So it began.

Brown's first choice for coach had been Frank Keaney, the originator of fast break basketball at Rhode Island State, the man from whom Auerbach's college had gotten this style of play. At the last minute, Keaney backed out over health issues, and Brown turned to "Honey" Russell, who had been successful at Seton Hall and who was a name in the college basketball world. From the beginning, however, it was a disaster. The team practiced in the Boston Arena Annex, a building Brown owned, and the players played on the second floor and slept on cots downstairs. Russell once said that on his first look at the place, the lighting was bad, it was cold, and one of the baskets had been hung upside down.

Welcome to professional basketball in Boston.

But it got worse.

That first training camp had been held when the Red Sox were playing the Cardinals in the '46 World Series, rendering the upstart Celtics beyond irrelevant. Their first game was held forty miles away in Rhode Island, against the Providence Steamrollers, and it received one paragraph in the *Boston Globe*, the story wedged between a schedule for Boston Park League football and Watertown's high school football win over Framingham. It was not exactly a commitment to this new professional team. But the *Globe* still did better than the *Boston Post*, which didn't cover the team for the first two seasons.

The team finished 22–38 in that first season, averaging about four thousand people in the Garden, which could seat 13,909 for basketball. And the only worthwhile thing that survived that first season of professional basketball was the parquet floor in the Boston Arena, made from leftover scraps of wood, due to the shortage of wood in World War II. A few years later, the parquet floor would be moved over to the Boston Garden, where it would become the most famous floor in all of basketball, the Celtics' signature.

But it wasn't in those fledgling years.

All it was then was a funny-looking court for a team that too few people cared about.

The other irony was that basketball was growing all over New England, even in the Boston Garden itself, which had sponsored a New England high school tournament since 1925, an event that brought the high school champions of the six New England states to the Garden every March. The games drew very well, as did the periodic Massachusetts high school tournaments that would also play in the Garden every March, games that always outdrew the Celtics back then.

Holy Cross had come out of virtual obscurity to win the national title in 1947, one of those incredible stories that seemed to defy belief. By a strange confluence of events, players coming back from the war being the biggest, Holy Cross had ended up with several New York City kids who brought their basketball expertise to a small Catholic school on a hill in Worcester, Massachusetts, forty miles west of Boston. Cousy had been a freshman on that team.

The Crusaders captured New England's imagination, even that of some of the Boston sportswriters. One of them dubbed them the "Fancy Pants A.C.," in homage to their showy style. Because they didn't have a real gym on campus, they played some of their games in a Worcester high school, some of them in the Boston Arena near Huntington Avenue, and the big ones in the Boston Garden, where they often played before large crowds. Invariably, they would play the first game of doubleheaders, traveling back and forth to Worcester in limousines, and most of the crowd would leave before the second game started, one featuring either Boston College or Harvard. Still, by the time Auerbach arrived in 1950, none of that had spilled over to the Celtics. Two coaches already had failed, and he knew that if he failed, too, he would be out of professional basketball forever. Brown had told him that in his first meeting with him, sugarcoating nothing. The word was Brown had already lost nearly half a million dollars on the team, and friends, and even his wife, were telling him to get out of the basketball business. But he believed professional basketball would work in Boston, and he had bought the team from the corporation that owned the Boston Garden.

All he had to do was educate the fans.

That had been part of Curt Gowdy's job description when he became the Celtics' broadcaster in those early years. His real job

was as the Red Sox' broadcaster, but he had been a college basketball star at Wyoming, and he had practically begged Gowdy to
do the Celtics, too.

In the beginning, before there were any television games,
Gowdy would even do some road games, although he never left
Boston. Instead, he would read a Western Union ticker and try to
"re-create" the game, complete with a picture of a basketball
court in front of him, and something that sounded like crowd
noise playing in the background.

Gowdy believed television was essential to growing the team's
popularity, even though Brown lived by the gate. Eventually, Auerbach sided with Gowdy, so Brown changed his mind and put a
Sunday afternoon game against the Knicks on television. But only
three thousand people showed up, and Brown went apoplectic.

"You're ruining me," said Brown. "Look at this crowd today."

"Walter," Gowdy pleaded, "we're on the air."

"I'm going to kill you when this game is over," Brown yelled.
"I should have never listened to you and Auerbach. I'm going to
go broke."

Gowdy tried to calm him down, but to no avail.

"I'll see you after the game," Brown continued. "You're fired.
I never want to see you again around a basketball."

But the next Sunday the Celtics had a much bigger crowd.

Walter Brown was beginning to like television.

But first he had to get the sportswriters to like the Celtics.

That had been why Cousy had been such a godsend back in
1950, even if Auerbach hadn't wanted him, referring to him, in
his infamous line, as a "local yokel."

It had been a telling comment at the time, a peek inside the
complicated personality of Arnold "Red" Auerbach. It had been

Auerbach at his abrasive worst, a public relations nightmare, for if you were a fledgling team trying to win over the hearts and minds of the local fans, wouldn't it have made sense to draft the local star?

Not to Red.

Who cared about a local yokel?

Not Red.

So from the beginning the Boston sportswriters didn't like him. They all loved Cousy, seeing him as someone the Celtics had been waiting for, someone who could put people in the seats, maybe even make the Celtics worth watching. So when Auerbach drafted six-foot-eleven Charlie Share out of Bowling Green instead of Cousy, they viewed it as the ultimate sacrilege.

Not that Auerbach didn't have his reasons. Cousy was a skinny six-foot-one guard in a game ruled by big men. The Celtics already had tried out several local college stars, and all had failed, including three of his former Holy Cross teammates. Maybe the biggest had been Tony Lavelli, the Yale star from nearby Somerville, where he had been a huge high school star, and who used to play the accordion at halftime while wearing his Celtics warm-ups, playing such things as "Lady of Spain," and selections from the William Tell Overture. So from a basketball perspective, the move certainly made sense. And for someone who so worshipped at the altar of control, the last thing Auerbach felt he needed was some little local star who threw the ball around his back and was loved by the adoring fans and the sportswriters, too, many of whom thought Holy Cross could beat the Celtics, an opinion that when expressed aloud would almost cause steam to come out of Auerbach's ears.

Or as he asked one day during a press conference back in the beginning, when once again the talk had turned to Cousy, "Walter, am I supposed to win, or am I supposed to please these guys?"

"Just win, Red," Brown said.

Not that Brown had a lot of choice.

By 1950 he needed a coach, and he needed some success. And when Auerbach became available, he relied on the advice of two men. One was Sammy Cohen, the sports editor of the *Boston Record*, who had sat near the Tri-Cities bench one night in the Garden when the Blackhawks had been in town. He had been impressed with both the way Auerbach had run his team and his obvious passion for the game. The other was Lou Pieri, the portly owner of the Rhode Island Auditorium in Providence, who wore dark suits and had slicked-back hair. Pieri had been impressed with Auerbach from the time years earlier when his Providence Steamrollers had been the worst team in the league, all but burning money, and he had asked Auerbach for an assessment of his team. Auerbach essentially told him he had no players, a lousy arena, and probably needed another half million just to be competitive. Pieri thanked him and closed down his team. Pieri said he would become a minority owner of the Celtics, providing an infusion of cash Brown so desperately needed, on one condition: Brown had to hire Auerbach.

So Auerbach now had his third pro team to coach. But it came with a caveat. If the Celtics didn't start winning, Brown would be out of the basketball business.

"When I walked out of Ben Kerner's office I was crushed," Auerbach once said. "I really was. Damn it. I had done a good job, but once again I had the rug pulled out from under me by circumstances I couldn't control. You can imagine what it meant to me the day I got the call from Walter Brown about the Celtics' situation. I didn't know Walter Brown at the time, but I had heard a lot of good things about the man. And the idea of working in Boston was particularly attractive because it meant I wouldn't be that far from home."

But there was no multiyear contract.

No security.

Just a chance.

If Auerbach showed his stubborn side with not drafting Cousy, it also showed he would do anything to win, even at the price of turning everyone against him.

That, too, would be at the cornerstone of what he was, this belief in winning above all else, even at the expense of his popularity as a young coach; his belief that he would do whatever he thought gave him the best chance to win, even if that upset people's feelings. It was why six years later he started five black players for a while, a first in the NBA. It was certainly a controversial move, yet one that had nothing to do with making a social statement and everything to do with trying to win games.

But Cousy had saved the Celtics in those early years, even if when Auerbach had finally wound up with him, the first thing he said was, "I hope you make it, but don't blame me if you don't. It's a big man's game."

"Boston was Red Sox country, Bruins country, and Cousy country," Heinsohn would often say.

One thing it wasn't was basketball country.

There were reasons for Cousy's huge popularity that transcended his Holy Cross days, the main one being that he wasn't some large man in short pants; he wasn't some behemoth as so often were the stars of the pro game back then, such as the George Mikans of the world. Cousy was Everyman; he looked like the guy who lived down the street, and he did things with a basketball few people had ever seen before, wondrous things that made basketball an art form. To see him in the middle of a fast break back then, teammates filling the lanes, and Cousy about to do some magician's trick with the ball, now you see it, now you don't, was to see the game's possibilities.

Was it any wonder he was so popular?

There was the belief by '57 that he had saved the league in those early years, that he was the biggest draw, the one who kept people moving through those turnstiles in all those old drafty arenas. And if it might have been overkill, there was no mistaking the reality that he got the most attention, had the most endorsements, started the first basketball camp, was finding more and more ways to market himself and take advantage of his fame, all those things he had learned in that spring seven years earlier with his "Bob Cousy All-Stars." In a sense, he was what the future NBA superstar would become.

He, too, had a rags-to-riches story, the kid who twice had been cut from his high school team in Queens. In fact, if he hadn't been discovered by the same coach, who already had cut him twice, playing a local rec league, his career could have died there in its infancy. Two years later was All-City. Still, it wasn't as if colleges were crawling all over him. A photo of the era shows a small skinny kid who almost looks as if he had snuck into the picture when no one was looking. His college choice came down to Boston College and Holy Cross, and that was only because someone from his hometown was playing at Holy Cross and tipped off Doggie Julian, the Holy Cross coach. He had known when he left for college that he really was leaving home for good. He had been conceived coming over on the boat from France, the only child of an introverted man who rarely expressed any emotion, and a mother who used to embarrass him as a child in stores in New York City when she would go on tirades about Germans. Even when they moved out of a New York City tenement to the more leafy world of Queens, it was a home where affection was seldom demonstrated, and he would always carry these hurts with him.

"I knew I wanted out of the house," he said. "I was seventeen and I was going to get away."

In the summer after his senior year in high school, he went to work in the Catskills, at a place called Tamarack Lodge, he and a high school teammate having been lured there by a man from Queens who coached the team there. The place looked like a Bavarian castle, complete with a pool and something called a planetarium. The Catskills were the epicenter of a summer basketball culture, a place where many college stars came to work as waiters during the day and then to play against the other lodges at night on outdoor courts, providing entertainment for the guests. The summer he was there, the Catskills were loaded with talent, including Mikan, Schayes, and Macauley, three of the biggest names in the college game, and surprisingly, Cousy held his own, foreshadowing what was to come.

"The games were very competitive," remembered Wes Field, Cousy's high school teammate who had gone to the Catskills with him. Field quickly realized that Cousy only got better as the competition got better. "The first game we played was against Neville Country Club with Schayes, who already was a big star at NYU, and the team from Klein's Hillside had practically the entire team from CCNY. There also were a few pros. But clearly Bob could play with anybody."

Tamarack Lodge was called a five-and-three-house, which in

the parlance of the Borscht Belt in the Catskills meant that wait-ers were to be tipped five dollars a week and busboys three. Cousy's job that summer was as a busboy, cleaning the tables and making sure the water glasses were full.

That and dancing with the girls after dinner.

But only with the ugly ones.

"That was the rule," said Cousy. "We were supposed to dance with the ugly girls so they would keep coming back to the lodge."

That fall he left for Holy Cross, and the beginning of a story no one could have made up.

For how could you make up his having gone in just thirteen years from being cut from his high school team to having become the biggest name in basketball? Or his having gotten to the Celt-ics due to the folding of a team called the Chicago Stags, three players put in a hat, Cousy among them, and Brown pulling his name out of that hat, Auerbach essentially being stuck with the local yokel?

By the mid-fifties, though, he was the star of the best offen-sive team in the NBA. Alongside him in the backcourt was Shar-man, who in the early seventies would coach the Los Angeles Lakers. But back then, a sweet-shooting guard who could shoot coming off screens and never missed an open shot, he was the perfect complement to Cousy.

Sharman was from Porterville, California, a town on the edge of the Central Valley. He had had one of those fabled high school careers, the three-sport star out of some adolescent novel, some-one who won two events in a track meet in the morning and pitched in the afternoon, and also had been a good enough tennis player to be in a national tournament while a senior in high school. He had gone to the University of Southern California, where he starred in both baseball and basketball. He was also on the bench for the Brooklyn Dodgers when they lost to the Giants and Bobby Thompson hit his famous home run in the 1951 play-off game.

Sharman had ended up with the Celtics almost by accident, but also because of Auerbach's ability to recognize talent. In 1950, playing both professional baseball and basketball, he was playing for the Washington Capitols, whose coach, Bones McKinney, didn't like to fly. The team would therefore take eighteen-hour train rides from Washington to Minneapolis, or they would drive, four to a car, sometimes even changing in the car.

This was professional sports?

"It was awful," Sharman said.

With the Celtics, he was the perfect backcourt partner. In today's basketball parlance, he would be the two guard and Cousy the point. Back then they were just guards, but Cousy always had the ball and Sharman never stopped moving. And when he was open, Cousy always got him the ball.

"Bob invented the point guard position," Sharman said.

They were the best backcourt in the game.

Sharman was a fitness aficionado, unheard of in those basketball days, when many players smoked, some even in the locker room before games, and weight lifting was widely considered bad for basketball players, the thinking being it would make them muscle-bound. He drank shakes he claimed gave him energy. He always had vitamins in his suitcase. He drank tea on the afternoon of games. He did calisthenics in front of his locker before games, as the rest of his teammates sat there and thought he was a wacko. He ran on days he wasn't practicing, sometimes jogging behind a car driven by his wife. And on the morning of game days, he would go to a local high school gym and shoot by himself, his way of preparing for the evening's game. Years later, as the Lakers' coach, he started doing this with the Lakers, much to the consternation of Lakers star Wilt Chamberlain who hated these "shootarounds." Today, virtually every college and NBA team in the country does morning shootarounds.

Sharman had note cards on his opponents, and every game day he would take a nap in the afternoon at exactly two o'clock. He was both meticulous and a perfectionist, to the point that when the Celtics played Horse, the age-old shooting game of having to match shots, Sharman never took a bad shot and almost never missed. He was so good at the game that his teammates grew tired of playing with him.

If their individual games were different, Sharman and Cousy were also similar. Both were perfectionists. Both placed winning above anything else. Both were extremely driven. Each admired the other, and they always roomed together on the road.

"I was always living out of my suitcase and he was always hanging up his clothes," Cousy said, "putting the same clothes in the same places in all the different rooms."

His nickname was "Easy Ed."

His name was Ed Macauley, and he was from St. Louis. He had been a hometown star at St. Louis University in the late forties, leading the hometown Billikens to the National Invitational Tournament championship in Madison Square Garden in 1948. He had transformed Billikens games from casual affairs attended by three hundred to four hundred people in a small gym into a crowd of eleven thousand that routinely showed up at the Municipal Auditorium. He also had been a star for the St. Louis Bombers of the old American Basketball Association until they folded in 1951. He was placed in the dispersal draft, and ended up with the Celtics. He was a skinny six foot eight, and to see pictures of him today conjures up such a different basketball world. But he could score, and that made him one of the league's certified stars.

In fact, he had been a bigger star than Cousy in college, and in January 1949, he had been on the cover of *Sport*, the biggest sports magazine in the country, published by McFadden's in New York City. "The slender, stoop-shouldered giant . . ." was how a profile article about him began. This was one more example that in the early years of the NBA, basketball was a game played not by your neighbor down the street, but by people thought of as giants.

"We always hoped he wouldn't be so tall because it might give him an inferiority complex, and we always hoped he'd study law and follow in his father's footsteps," his mother said in the magazine article.

Macauley was an instant star on the Celtics, their only real inside scorer, easily adapting to Auerbach's fast-paced style. He could run and he could shoot, and if he struggled on the boards against many of the stronger and rougher centers, there was nothing he could do about that.

As was typical of the times, he didn't live in Boston year round, he and his wife renting a house in nearby Revere Beach for the season, then returning back to St. Louis every summer. He saw Boston as a place where he made his living, not his home, and though he liked the city, it was not a place to which he was emotionally connected. He certainly liked his teammates, especially

Cousy, who passed him the ball, but he was not particularly close to any of them. Nor was he close to Auerbach, whom he considered a good coach, but not the best one.

"Red had an ego, and he was the boss, there was no question about that," he said. "No one crossed him. You didn't win then in the pros because of coaches. They could cause you to lose, but not to win."

So the Celtics had three guys who were very skilled offensively, including the most popular player in the game. They played a fast-breaking style that generated a lot of points. The three scorers were surrounded by a bunch of role players, guys like Bob Brannum, Dick Hemric, Jack Nichols, who subordinated themselves to Cousy, Sharman, and Macauley. They were all veterans, big strong guys who were never going to beat too many guys down the court. Hemric was called "Old Oak Legs" for his lack of mobility. Brannum was the enforcer, the role he eventually would hand down to Loscutoff, like the passing of a family heirloom. He had gone to Michigan State, and he had come of age in professional basketball by riding trains throughout the Midwest. He was a tough, no-pretense guy. In those early years, the NBA was full of guys like him.

During the fall in Auerbach's early years when they were always playing exhibition games throughout New England, another night another game, Brannum became infamous for going into some little diner in the middle of nowhere and ordering a steak.

"Okay, honey," he'd tell the waitress. "Go out and get a steer, knock off its horns, wipe its ass, and run it in here."

He might have been listed in the program as a forward, but his real job was to protect Cousy, who was forever being pushed and grabbed and knocked down, especially in those early years before the 24-second clock when the Celtics would have a lead and Cousy would just dribble around and kill the clock, using both his quickness and great ball-handling ability to get around slower guards, before someone would simply all but tackle him to stop the clock.

One of them was a guard named Paul Hoffman, who went by the nickname of "Bear." As the story goes, the teams had played a game in Baltimore on a Saturday night, and then both of them rode a train all night to play Sunday afternoon in the Boston Garden; such were the vagaries of the NBA schedule. So there was Cousy guarding Hoffman when the Bear decided to barrel to the basket.

"Let him go," Hoffman whispered. "Let him go."

Cousy stepped aside like a matador escaping a charging bull, only to see Brannum move up and hit Hoffman in the throat with a forearm. When Hoffman got up, he ran the length of the court on his way to Auerbach.

"You son of a bitch," he yelled. "You told him to do it."

"You're damn right I did," Auerbach shot back.

With Auerbach it was very simple: Beat up on one of my stars, and one of my guys will take your head off. There was nothing ever subtle about Red Auerbach.

The Celtics led the league in scoring in 1956 for the third straight year. They were the NBA's best show, the most entertaining team, and not one season had ended with Auerbach thinking his team had underachieved.

The only problem?

They couldn't stop anybody.

And they didn't rebound very well.

"Macauley was built more like a small forward," Cousy said, "but he was forced to be our center."

So defense and rebounding were the two Achilles' heels that prevented them from being a great team. These had been the reason they kept losing to the Syracuse team, as the Nats were both tougher and played a more physical style, plus it was so very hard to beat them in Syracuse. Auerbach had long known he had to get better defensively. He recognized that this particular team had gone as far as it could go, its deficiencies being physical ones. He knew nothing was ever going to change unless he could upgrade his roster; otherwise, his fate would always be to watch someone else get to the NBA Finals because someone else would always be on top of the basketball world where Auerbach so desperately yearned to be.

Enter Heinsohn.

Enter Bill Russell.

Enter the Celtics as we've come to know them.

Enter the dawning of a new America.

CHAPTER SIX

f the Celtics didn't know just what they were getting in Russell, they thought they knew with Heinsohn. He also had been drafted in the spring of '56, the Celtics having his rights under something called the territorial draft, a rule that said an NBA team held the draft rights to any college player within a fifty-mile radius. It was a rule meant to increase interest in the NBA game, the idea being that local college stars would, if nothing else, be a gate attraction, no small thing in a league trying to survive.

The drafting of Heinsohn, who had been a huge star at Holy Cross and a first-team all-American, was vintage Auerbach. He had started in Heinsohn's junior year telling the Boston media that, yeah, that big kid Heinsohn out there in Worcester had talent, but he had flaws, too.

"The kid is lackadaisical," he said. "He doesn't hustle. He doesn't have the right attitude. He doesn't have the proper temperament. He doesn't mix it up under the boards. And he can't play for me with all that baby fat on him. This guy's got no business weighing 235. But when you're a big star in college you get to thinking you're indispensable, that you can do any damned thing you want. Well, that doesn't go up here."

So Heinsohn had come to believe the Celtics didn't want him. He knew little about Auerbach, other than from seeing him yell and carry on at a couple of exhibition games the Celtics had played in Worcester. Heinsohn had thought then that Auerbach didn't seem like a very nice person. And, oh yeah, Auerbach liked to smoke cigars. And now Auerbach was demeaning him in the press, denigrating him as a player. Auerbach had done essentially the same thing to Cousy six years earlier; it was his way of putting young players in their place right from the beginning and, as his little slice of psychological warfare, letting them know who was the boss. Heinsohn, however, didn't know that. All he knew was that the Celtics didn't seem very interested in him. Consequently, at one point he considered going to play for the Peoria Caterpillars in AAU basketball, a move he saw as an alternative to the NBA; AAU basketball provided a decent job along with playing for the team.

"They're interested in you," Cousy told him one day over the telephone.

"They have some way of showing it," Heinsohn said.

"Forget what you read in the papers," Cousy said. "They are interested in you and they want to see you."

Heinsohn didn't really know Cousy, even though they had met once when the Celtics were playing an exhibition game in the Worcester Auditorium, and they both had played for Buster Sheary at Holy Cross.

But Cousy said he would drive him to Boston.

"What kind of contract should I ask for?" Heinsohn said.

"Make your own deal," Cousy said.

He did. He met with Auerbach and Brown in the Boston Garden and signed for $9,000 a year for two years.

"Okay," Auerbach said after Heinsohn had signed his contract, puffing on his ever-present cigar, "you're with us now, right kid? I'm going to tell you right now. Take that T-shirt you wear under your uniform and shove it. You're a Celtic now." Heinsohn had always worn a white T-shirt under his Holy Cross uniform in college games.

Heinsohn was six foot seven, with blond hair worn in a brush cut. Very skilled for his size, he offered another little preview of what the game was evolving into. He could put the ball on the floor, he could pass, and he had grown up playing a lot of positions, so he was versatile, too. In one of life's little ironies, however, Heinsohn would be remembered more for his years as a Celtics broadcaster than he would for his years as a player; he was a victim of the passage of time, the era he played in, and having been a broadcaster far longer than he was a player. But Heinsohn was a Hall of Fame player, one of the first of the talented, multidimensional forwards doing their part to change the NBA game.

He grew up in Union City, New Jersey, on the other side of the tunnel from the glittering spires of Manhattan, the son of a man who had worked for the National Biscuit Company and a mother who worked in the local Woolworth's. His father had lost his job during the Depression. Then World War II came along, and the young Heinsohn learned another lesson in life's grim realities. Because he was of German descent, the neighborhood kids began calling him a Nazi, taunting him in grammar school.

"I had to fight my way home every day," he said.

This eventually ended when his father told him to pick out the biggest kid and fight him.

But maybe the most important lesson he learned then was that he couldn't depend on others for either his happiness or his sense of self-worth.

"I learned to operate in my own peer group," he said. "I learned to create my own world."

One of the ways he did this was by teaching himself to draw, and his art would remain a passion for the rest of his life. So at a young age, Heinsohn became both an artist and a competitive basketball player, two things that always would define his life.

He had been a high school all-American, a team picked by Haskell Cohen, then the NBA's public relations director. It had been announced in *Parade* magazine, which was in innumerable Sunday newspapers across the country. He played in the North-South All-Star Game, and several big-name coaches came to his house to recruit him. He visited North Carolina State, had a tryout at Niagara, and probably could have gone anywhere he wanted, as college recruiting was beginning to become more sophisticated, especially for kids who were six foot seven with a plethora of offensive skills. He decided on Holy Cross because both Togo Palazzi and Earl Markey, who had had great careers at Holy Cross, had been from New Jersey. He went to college thinking he might want to be a doctor.

He also had been someone with a definite sense of self as a basketball player, someone very confident in his ability. Part of that, certainly, was that he had come of age in a great basketball environment; he had even been the MVP of a postseason tournament, as a sophomore in high school no less, one that had included both college players and adults. He used to spend summers in both high school and college playing competitive pickup games in Palisades Park in north Jersey, games that were all about keeping the court, to the point that if you lost, you might as well go swimming in the nearby pool because you weren't going to be playing basketball for a while.

He had been the MVP of the 1954 National Invitational Tournament in Madison Square Garden when only a sophomore, had had great success as a college player, and once had an amazing 51 points and 42 rebounds in a game against Boston College. He also had a great attitude about the game, and the vagaries of it, something he had learned as a high school player.

In a championship game on the road he had been fouled, and he had to make two key free throws to keep his team in the game.

Everyone was booing.

He was nervous.

What if he missed?

Somehow he was able to block it all out, all the noise, all the pressure, all of it, and tell himself that he was either going to be the hero or the goat, and that either way he was able to deal with both scenarios.

That had become his personal creed: The ball was either going to go in or out; it was just basketball. Heinsohn never lacked for confidence.

And from the beginning he was instantly successful with the Celtics and had no trouble adjusting to the NBA. He could run well enough to fit into the Celtics' fast-paced style. He knew no fear and was not hesitant about getting up shots, even if the older players constantly kidded him about it. Cousy was forever needling him about it during all those rides from Worcester to Boston, but no matter. He even occasionally would take hook shots from the right-hand corner, something no one had ever done, and something no one has done since.

The point is that Heinsohn was never a bashful rookie. He arrived with a strong sense of self, the legacy of having had to defend himself from the barbs and neighborhood kids as a child. He took a lot of shots, and if any of his teammates complained, he took some more. Knicks star Dick McGuire said he never saw a rookie as cocky as Heinsohn.

He soon was called "Tommy Gun" because he shot so much. But so what? This was the way he always had played, and this was the way he was going to play now. And there was no denying his ability. He had a flat jump shot, which he got off quickly, as though it was being cocked from behind his head, the legacy of playing as a kid in a little gym in Jersey with a low ceiling. He had the hook shot. Often, it seemed as if he had a shot for every occasion. So what if he sometimes took a bad shot or two? Cousy said the only time Heinsohn shot was when he had the ball.

He also quickly learned that Cousy was as good as advertised, maybe better.

"He was a one-man offense," Heinsohn often said through the years. "The only time we ever called a play was maybe coming out of a time-out. We never called one coming up the floor. Cooz just ran things. He would make things happen. If you got a half step on your man, he would get you the ball. And if you weren't running as hard as he wanted you to early in the game, he'd throw the ball just off your fingertips to make you run harder."

Heinsohn also had one other characteristic essential to the Celtics: He was Auerbach's whipping boy, right there with Loscutoff, Auerbach's other target.

Not that Loscutoff, the six-foot-five bruiser from the University of Oregon who was the Celtics' so-called hatchet man, particularly liked it. Late in his career, when asked what he wanted to do when he retired, he said, "Get Auerbach in an alley."

Heinsohn was always too heavy, too lazy, too something. But he quickly came to realize that Auerbach was never going to yell at either Cousy or Russell, nor was he going to yell at Sharman, who had a bit of a temper and might just haul off and punch Auerbach in the face. Nor was he ever going to yell at Frank Ramsey, who was very sensitive and might just take it to heart. So he yelled at Heinsohn and Loscutoff, the two guys he figured could take it. That was another tenet of Auerbach's coaching style, his belief that all players were different. Some had to be prodded; some had to be encouraged. He would rant and rave at his players collectively, but he motivated them individually, intuitively knowing what buttons to push, who needed to be stroked, who needed to be whipped. He coached with his instincts, not out of some old dog-eared coaching manual.

"When he wanted to get on someone to stir up things in the dressing room he got on me," Heinsohn said. "He knew I could take it. I was his whipping boy. I understood what he was doing."

So it was when Auerbach lit into him at halftime, even though he already had scored 20 points.

"Red, what the hell have I done wrong tonight?" Heinsohn finally asked in exasperation.

Auerbach looked at him with a serious face.

"Tommy," he said. "You warmed up lousy."

It was always Heinsohn's fault, Loscutoff's fault. They were the ones not getting back quickly enough on defense. They were the ones not boxing out well enough. They were the ones not running wind sprints hard enough. Heinsohn was the one smoking too many cigarettes, the one not doing his push-ups when Auerbach's back was turned. He was the one always committing some little sin, some basketball sacrilege; it was as if Auerbach knew he could yell at the entire team by yelling at Heinsohn.

This was the way it was throughout Heinsohn's career, Auerbach once saying that Heinsohn had the "oldest twenty-seven-year-old body in the history of sports."

By the spring of his rookie year, Auerbach was saying he always knew what he was getting in Heinsohn, that he always had regarded him as a sleeper, one of the reasons why he felt he could live without Macauley. He felt that because Heinsohn was younger and stronger than Macauley, he would be a better rebounder. But to have a rookie this talented? A rookie who had had little adjustment to the NBA, no matter how much Auerbach made him a whipping boy?

No one expected that.

"I just wanted about nine or ten rebounds a game from him," he said. "I didn't expect him in one year to equal Macauley's offensive output."

But from the beginning, Heinsohn quickly came to know Auerbach was a master manipulator, never motivating the different players the same way, but a puppeteer whose only goal was to make the group better, whatever it took.

He is now recognized as the greatest winner in the history of American sport, not to mention the first black coach in NBA history, but in the winter of 1956 the basketball world was divided on Bill Russell.

No matter that the year before he had led the San Francisco

Bill Russell, who came to the Celtics in December 1956, straight from the Olympic team.

Courtesy of the Boston Herald

Russell and his wife, Rose, greeted at Boston's Logan Airport by Celtics guard Bill Sharman and the team's owner, Walter Brown.

The Sports Museum

Boston Garden, the legendary original home of the Celtics, which opened in 1929 on Causeway Street.

Steve Babineau/Getty Images

Bill Russell holding a sweater with the Celtics logo. Russell played for the team from December 1956 through April 1969, winning eleven titles.

Courtesy of the Boston Herald

Tommy Heinsohn, the 6'7" rook
forward from Holy Cross Colleg
who had thirty-seven points in t
seventh game of the NBA fina

NBA Photos/Getty Ima

Never known for being shy, Celtics coach Red Auerbach with his omnipresent rolled-up program.

The Sports Museum

Bob Cousy, the era's "Mr. Basketball," throwing one of his trademark passes against the Hawks.

Richard Meek/Getty Images

Arnie Risen, a Celtics veteran who befriended Bill Russell and helped him to make his transition to the NBA.

The Sports Museum

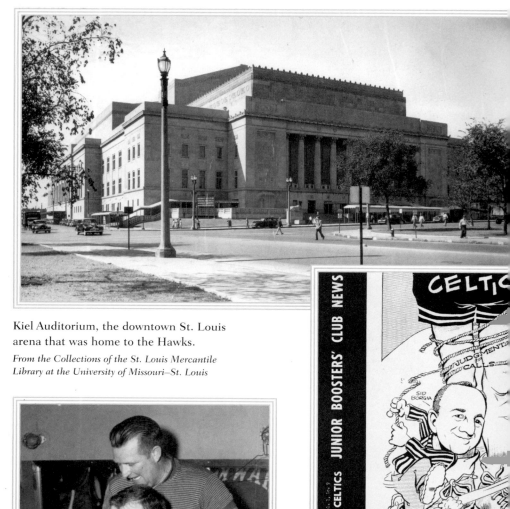

Kiel Auditorium, the downtown St. Louis
arena that was home to the Hawks.

*From the Collections of the St. Louis Mercantile
Library at the University of Missouri–St. Louis*

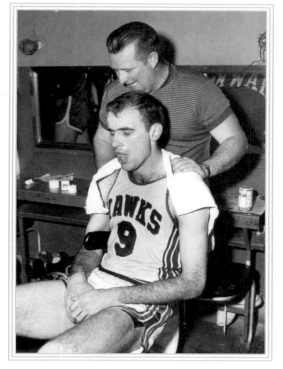

Sid Borgia, longtime
Celtics nemesis, seen tying
the legs of the Celtics.

The Sports Museum

Hawks star player Bob Pettit,
a Hall of Famer and one of the
best players of his era.

*From the Collections of the St. Louis
Mercantile Library at the University of
Missouri–St. Louis*

The Hawks' Bob Pettit on the floor,
flanked by teammate Jack Coleman
(*left*) and the Celtics' Arnie Risen.
The referee is Arnie Heft.

From the Collections of the St. Louis
Mercantile Library at the University of
Missouri–St. Louis

St. Louis Hawks' owner, Ben Kerner,
who lived and died with his team.

From the Collections of the
St. Louis Mercantile Library at the
University of Missouri–St. Louis

Bill Russell and Cliff
Hagan duel for a rebound.
Richard Meek/Getty Images

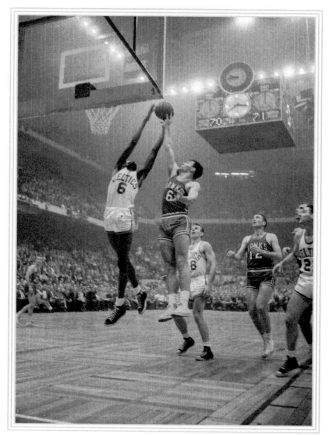

Auerbach takes issue with
a referee's call as Cousy
(*center right*) and Heinsohn
(*center left*) look on.
Robert Riger/Getty Images

Ben Kerner with his mother (*center*) and Bob Pettit's mother.
Kerner's mother attended every game and Pettit's mother periodically
made the trip to St. Louis from Baton Rouge, Louisiana.
From the Collections of the St. Louis Mercantile Library at the University of Missouri–St. Louis

Tom Heinsohn after fouling out in game seven at the Boston Garden.
The Sports Museum

Bill Sharman being honored in the Boston Garden as his wife looks on.
The Sports Museum

Exuberant Celtics fans carry Tom Heinsohn off the court following the Celtics' first NBA title.
The Sports Museum

Dons to the NCAA title, or that he seemed poised to do it again, or that he would finish his senior season having won fifty-five straight games and back-to-back national titles. No matter that he seemed to get every rebound, or that he could seemingly block shots at will. The knock on him as a college player was that he scored only on layups and dunks.

This was someone who was going to be a great pro?

Some people in the game didn't think so, seeing him as just another version of Walter Dukes, the tall, thin black center who had been in the league for a few undistinguished years. Johnny Kundla, who had coached the Lakers to four NBA titles, derisively said Russell couldn't hit a shot past two feet. Russell also supposedly had moped around in a practice session before the East-West All-Star game in Madison Square Garden, to the point that Lester Harrison, owner of the Rochester Royals, who had the first pick, had his doubts about just how effective Russell would be in the NBA.

But Bill Reinhart, Auerbach's old college coach, had seen Russell play at the All-College Tournament in Oklahoma City in December 1955 and told Auerbach he had to get him, that Russell could give the Celtics the one thing they didn't have—the missing piece. He said Russell could run and rebound and block shots, just what the Celtics needed. This was not insignificant. Auerbach had been greatly influenced by Reinhart. In fact, his entire offensive philosophy was Reinhart's. And Reinhart's message had been reinforced by Pete Newell, a well-regarded college coach on the West Coast whom Auerbach knew: He had to get this kid, Russell, whatever it took.

There was virtually no scouting of college players then by professional teams. College games, even the NCAA finals, were not on national television. So much of the drafting of players was based on hearsay and reputation. Or else it was by referral, Auerbach's calling up someone he trusted who had seen a certain player. And because he had spent time in the basketball world of summers in the Catskills, and often traveled around the country to lead coaching clinics, he was well connected in the basketball world.

So it was with Russell.

Auerbach also asked Don Barksdale, the second black player to ever play for the Celtics, to check out this Russell for him. Barksdale had played his college ball at UCLA and lived in California.

"He can't shoot at all, but he's the best basketball player I've ever seen," Barksdale reported back.

That was enough for Auerbach.

But he had a problem.

The Celtics owned the third pick in the '56 NBA Draft.

So how was he going to get Russell?

The Rochester Royals had the first pick. They were owned by Lester Harrison, another man who owned the building his team played in, another man who had financial problems, another man for whom the bottom line had become more important than the record.

Enter Brown, who, as the story goes, offered Harrison a great deal on some future Ice Capades appearances. Later, Harrison would refute this, saying he passed on Russell because he knew he didn't want to play in Rochester. Whatever the reason, he agreed not to draft Russell. Instead, he selected six-foot-two Sihugo Green of Duquesne with the number one pick in the '56 NBA Draft.

That left St. Louis, which had the second pick.

So how was Auerbach going to get the Hawks' pick, especially given that the Hawks were owned by Kerner, the man who had feuded with Auerbach in the Tri-Cities?

So began the machinations for the trade that changed the NBA's history.

It began with a simple premise: St. Louis was a segregated city and might not have been the best match for Russell. Or at least St. Louis might have had a few misgivings about drafting him at a time when the year before a black woman named Rosa Parks had refused to sit in the back on a bus in Montgomery, Alabama, the incident that began the civil rights movement and began the public career of a twenty-six-year-old minister from Atlanta named Martin Luther King who led the protest marches in Montgomery.

Would St. Louis in 1957 have been ready for Bill Russell, even though they had had a black player on their roster the year before, though he rarely played?

That remains one of basketball history's great unanswered questions.

Russell also had reportedly turned down an offer from the Globetrotters, and Kerner, who always was dancing along a financial precipice, was no doubt concerned about how much Russell would demand. The word was he wanted at least $25,000, and there was no way Kerner was going to give him that, not for some skinny Negro center who people were saying couldn't shoot, no matter how many college games he won. Who was going to pay money to see him play—and in St. Louis, no less? Kerner had enough problems trying to make the Hawks work in St. Louis without bringing in some Negro rookie.

But nor was he going to give Auerbach anything for nothing.

Kerner's initial asking price was Macauley, the St. Louis native. Now that was someone who could sell tickets in St. Louis, the hometown hero. That was someone the people would come out to see. That was someone who made sense to Kerner, and Kerner was nothing if not pragmatic.

"Ben was the most underrated promoter of all of them," said Jack Levitt, a former minor-league baseball player who went to work for the Hawks when they came to St. Louis in 1955, and did just about everything, at various times running the 24-second clock, working at the scorer's table, and eventually doing scouting of college players in the South where he often would travel in his real job for a consumer finance company. "He wasn't really a basketball guy—not in the beginning, anyway. But he knew how to run a business, how to hustle, and he knew what people wanted. The Hawks only had a staff of about four people then, but Ben made going to a Hawks' game in St. Louis a big deal, an event."

And now he knew the St. Louis fans wanted Macauley.

But it was a high price for the Celtics, given that Macauley was the Celtics' only inside scorer. He also was well liked by everyone, especially by Brown, who told Auerbach he wouldn't do the deal unless Macauley agreed to it.

Brown not only owned the Celtics; he had grown to love them, too. And for those first years, all they did was eat his money, Brown at one point having to mortgage his house and sell off some of his Ice Capades stock to keep the team alive. But he had been one of the founding fathers of the league in 1946, and he believed in basketball, calling it a sport that had been around for a half century but had never been promoted the way it should have been. So he believed in the Celtics, and he believed in Auerbach, and he always was loyal to the players. All of them soon came to know it was better to negotiate with Brown than with Auerbach. All of them came to know they were playing for a great owner, to the point that one time, a few years earlier, he hadn't had enough money to pay the players their play-off shares, but they respected him so much that they all had waited patiently until the following year to get it.

His only real flaw was a temper, something he always was later apologizing for, such as the time late in the season when he blasted the team for losing a game to Syracuse, only to come into the locker room the next day and apologize. Or the time he called them all "chokers" after another loss, only to apologize for that remark, too.

So it definitely was in character for Brown to make sure Macauley was willing to go home to St. Louis before he signed off on the trade.

Macauley did.

First and foremost, it was the opportunity to go home to St. Louis, where he'd always been a hometown favorite. Second, he had a nine-year-old son who had spinal meningitis, and he believed that being back home in St. Louis would be better for his family. In fact, given his son's needs, there was even a question that Macauley might decide not to come back to Boston the following year, anyway.

"You would be doing me a favor if you traded me to St. Louis," Macauley told Brown.

But just when Auerbach thought he had a deal, Kerner upped the ante. He also wanted Hagan, the six-foot-four Kentucky all-American whom the Celtics had drafted in the third round in 1953. Hagan had played another year of college after that, and was coming off a two-year army stint included in the deal. Auerbach didn't like the idea of losing Hagan, considering it one more example of Kerner's always trying to put something over on him.

"Red, I need bodies," Kerner told Auerbach. "Macauley is not enough. It's Hagan and Macauley or no deal."

So it became the deal: Macauley and Hagan to the Hawks for the second pick in the NBA Draft.

Not that Auerbach really knew what he was getting. And now he had lost Macauley.

Then he saw Russell play.

In Washington in the spring of '56, Russell was playing at an exhibition game for the Olympic team, which would play in the fall in Melbourne. Auberbach and Brown went down to see him.

"It was the first time I had ever seen the kid play and he stunk out the joint," Auerbach would later say. "No offense, no defense, nothing. They had some high school kids on the other team and they looked better than my guy. I looked at Walter and he looked at me, and neither of us said a word.

"Then a great thing happened. I had invited Russell and a couple of his friends to have dinner with Walter and me at my house after the game. We got there first and waited. Pretty soon they arrived and the first thing Russell did was stick his hand toward me and say, 'I'm sorry.'"

"For what?" Auerbach asked.

"For the way I played tonight. I don't usually play that way. It's the worst I ever played in my life and I'm sorry you had to see it."

Had he been nervous?

Had he been sick?

Why had Russell been so bad?

Whatever the reason, he was apologizing.

He also was getting one of his first introductions to Auerbach's style.

"If you do," Auerbach replied, "you better stay in Melbourne because I won't be in Boston. I'll be back coaching junior high in Brooklyn."

CHAPTER SEVEN

Russell was not the Celtics' first black player. That distinction had gone to Chuck Cooper, who had played his college ball at Duquesne and whom they had drafted with the first pick of the second round in 1950.

"Walter, don't you know that he's a colored boy?" one of the other owners had said to Brown.

"I don't give a damn if he's striped, polka dot, or plaid," Brown shot back. "The Boston Celtics take Charles Cooper of Duquesne."

Soon after the Celtics chose Cooper, Knicks boss Ned Irish signed Nat "Sweetwater" Clifton of the Harlem Globetrotters, so named because he drank a lot of soda pop, which he referred to as "sweet water." But the first African-American to actually play in an NBA game was Earl Lloyd, a forward from West Virginia State, who had been selected in the ninth round, but whose Washington Capitols opened their season one night before both the Celtics and the Knicks.

It had been three years since Jackie Robinson had integrated baseball, but professional basketball's integration in 1950 took place almost quietly, with none of the demonstrable hate and public fervor that had accompanied Robinson's entrance into the Major Leagues. One theory was that basketball players had been to college and didn't seem to harbor the same vitriol against blacks as did many baseball players, most of whom had not gone to college. Many baseball players had also grown up in the South. Another theory was that college basketball had long been integrated in much of the country, so most players had played against blacks before.

Still another theory was that so few people seemed to care about the NBA that anything happening in it was almost irrelevant.

Also to consider was a history of black players in professional basketball dating back to the early years of the century. The New York Rens, a black team named after the Renaissance Casino Ballroom in Harlem, a place where the likes of Count Basie and Duke Ellington used to play, had started in 1923, in the middle of the Harlem Renaissance. They often played against white teams of the era, and when they played home games, people danced before games, during halftime, and after games. They were a serious team, and toured throughout the Midwest and South in a bus they called the Grey Goose. Their history was a story of prejudice and discrimination, their road secretary carrying a pistol and forever telling the players not to go on the court until he had the money. They eventually joined the National Basketball League, but by 1949 they were done.

Then there were the Globetrotters, born in 1927, the baby of Abe Saperstein, a white guy who had coached both youth teams in Chicago and an all-black team called the Savoy Big Five, named after a dance hall. He took his new black team on the road, initially calling them Saperstein's New York, before changing the name to the Harlem Globetrotters, in homage to Harlem's being the symbolic home of blacks in the United States. He dressed them in red, white, and blue uniforms and took them on the road. They played in dance halls. They played in warehouses. They played in livestock barns. They played in ole opry houses. They played virtually anywhere Saperstein thought he could get a date. They even once played in a drained swimming pool.

"We earned just enough to get to the next town, but never enough to get back home," Saperstein once said.

By the late forties, they were the most famous basketball team in the world. In 1948, two years after the NBA had been formed, they beat the NBA champion Lakers and George Mikan before eighteen thousand people in Chicago Stadium. They often appeared in NBA arenas, almost always outdrawing the pro teams, their clowning and tricks showcasing basketball as entertainment. Because of that, Saperstein had tremendous clout with the NBA owners. But the NBA was robbing the Globetrotters of their stature. "Sweetwater" Clifton's jumping to the Knicks in 1950 had been symbolic, a sign that black players were looking at the NBA, some of them no longer wanting to essentially be seen as a vaudeville act. Some of the owners feared this, especially Eddie Gottlieb in Philadelphia, whose roots went way back in the game, and who warned his fellow owners that if this trend continued, Saperstein would not be pleased, and this wouldn't bode well for any of them.

Is it any wonder Saperstein had made a big push for Russell when he was coming out of college?

As the story goes, when he met with Saperstein, the Globetrotters' owner kept talking to Russell's adviser, not him. Russell hadn't liked that, feeling that Saperstein had thought he wasn't intelligent enough to make decisions for himself. There had been rumors that Saperstein was going to offer Russell the amazing salary of $50,000 a year, more than double what Cousy reportedly was making, but that when the negotiations actually began, Saperstein was offering far less. In retrospect, it's impossible to imagine that Russell was ever going to put himself in a situation where he was going to play the clown to white audiences, but who knew that back in '56? Regardless, Russell wasn't interested.

Yet if the advent of blacks into professional basketball was less dramatic than it had been in baseball, that didn't mean the early racial pioneers in the NBA didn't go through their own racial hell, to one degree or another. If many of the players didn't seem to have problems playing against black players, that didn't mean many fans welcomed black players into the NBA. Case in point was the treatment Russell received in St. Louis—that, and the problems black players had in Southern cities throughout the fifties and sixties while playing exhibition games. An incident illustrating such problems occurred in the early sixties when Russell and the other black players on the Celtics refused to play a game in Lexington, Kentucky, because of discriminatory practices in the city.

Cooper's experience came in 1950 when the Celtics had an exhibition game in Raleigh, North Carolina. The South was still segregated then, and Cooper couldn't stay in the same hotel with his teammates, couldn't eat in the same restaurants, couldn't even go to the same movie theater. After the game, the plan was to fly to New York the next morning, but Cousy was concerned about where Cooper was going to spend the night.

"He's taking a train out tonight," Auerbach said.

"Can I go with him?" Cousy asked.

"Yes," Auerbach said.

The train was scheduled to come through Raleigh at three in the morning, so Cousy and Cooper walked around, killing time. At one point they went to a package store near the train station to get some beer for the long ride north. Eventually, they went looking for a restroom, only to find one marked WHITE, the other marked COLORED. Cousy was embarrassed and didn't know what to say. For the first time in his life he felt ashamed to be white, as his eyes filled with tears. If he always had known discrimination was wrong and had been offended as a child when his mother had made derogatory remarks about Germans in a New York store, this was the first time he had seen its effects.

He had grown up in New York City feeling like an outsider, called "Flenchy" by kids in the neighborhood, because he rolled his r's and had a minor speech impediment. He always had been ashamed of his home life, of having grown up an only child in a house where there was little display of affection, a home he had essentially left as soon as he graduated from high school. He always had been sensitive to those who were different, those who were constantly battling for acceptance, and now he was seeing it firsthand. He felt powerless.

They waited for the train in silence.

"All night we studiously avoided the subject," he said. "I felt as though I was at a wake. Finally I spoke up. 'The colored aren't the only ones who are persecuted,' I said. 'Hitler persecuted the Jews and so did a lot of others. And I was reading in the papers where they threw bombs at Catholic churches somewhere in Louisiana not long ago.'

"Chuck looked at me for a minute. Then he said quietly, 'That's all right, but you can't tell a Jew or a Catholic by looking at him.' I changed the subject quickly."

The Celtics' second black player was Barksdale, who played for two years in the early fifties and shared an apartment in Kenmore Square with Johnny Most. He was from UCLA, a light-skinned man who later would become a record producer in California, but both Cooper and Barksdale had been role players, with minimum impact.

Russell was different.

Not just in stature, but in attitude.

Part of the Celtics' culture was the rookies carrying the ball bags, something Heinsohn always did while Russell was off with the Olympic team. So when Russell arrived, Heinsohn just assumed Russell would start to carry the ball bags.

Sorry.

Not Russell. Another part of Celtics' culture was the rookies fetching sodas for the veteran players. Not Russell. Part of Celtics' culture was the rookies paying for cabs and being reimbursed by Auerbach later. Not Russell. He would do none of these things, would do nothing that might make him look subservient. In fact, he would do nothing he didn't want to do, including sign autographs, something Heinsohn quickly discovered.

The Celtics were in Madison Square Garden to play the Knicks, and Heinsohn was going around having his new teammates sign a program for his family, who had come in from nearby Jersey for the game.

"You know I don't sign autographs," Russell said when Heinsohn approached him.

"I know, Russ," Heinsohn said, "but this is for my cousin."

"No," Russell said.

Bill Russell didn't sign autographs.

Nor was he going to go out of his way for Heinsohn that first year. They had been rivals of sorts the year before in college, Heinsohn being called the best player on the East Coast and Russell the best player on the West Coast. Now they were both rookies, Heinsohn the hometown boy from Holy Cross, and if not as beloved as Cousy had been in college, certainly another fan favorite. Did Russell resent this at some level?

Who knows?

Later, Russell would say that first year he wasn't particularly close to anyone on the team, that he had arrived late, and had arrived guarded. This was not surprising. He had been born in Louisiana, in the segregated South, leaving for California when he was nine because his father believed there were more opportunities there. He had grown up hearing stories of how his grandfather hadn't had the chance to get an education, how his father had gone to a colored school as a child, had worked in a paper bag factory in something called a "Negro job." He had heard the story of the time his mother went into town in a new dress, only to have a cop say, "Who do you think you are, nigger, a white woman? Get out of town before sundown, or I'll throw you in jail."

He had ridden in the colored section of the train from Louisiana to St. Louis with his mother and brother. His brother had been arrested as a child for selling newspapers in a "whites only" section. Racism had been part of the air he had breathed as a child.

In his first book, he provided the following insight:

You are little, but you learn fast. Be off the street by five o'clock. Move fast if you are little and black. Keep moving.

Because the police will get you and book you and maybe kick you. Because you are black. And a child wonders: Why did they do that? What does it make me? Am I nothing? Am I a non-person?

He went on:

The Negro learns to hate authority. And the Negro learns also to hate himself. They are taught through repetition that they are the scum of the earth and they are bad. They have nothing in common with anyone, not even each other. . . . They become more and more frustrated. They lose respect for themselves, and they lose respect for society. Pretty soon you develop a hatred for yourself. And then you lose all association. This is what happened to the Negro in this time, and in this place.

These were the scars Russell took with him wherever he went, the personal baggage he always carried, through all the games and all the college fame. Whenever he thought he might have moved past all that baggage, somehow there was always another reminder. One such experience was the time in college when he'd been invited to the White House by President Dwight Eisenhower, part of a select group of superstar athletes such as Cousy, baseball greats Willie Mays and Hank Greenberg, and boxers Archie Moore and Gene Tunney. Afterward, he had gone back to visit relatives in Louisiana, where in harsh contrast to his White House experience, he was treated as "just another black boy, just so much dirt, with no element of human courtesy or decency shown to me or mine."

Even at the University of San Francisco, amidst all the wins and all the acclaim, race and the perceptions about it always had been part of the equation. He had grown up in a housing project in Oakland, across the bay from San Francisco. There were few black students on the USF campus, and when the team started three of them, a segment of alumni didn't like it. Russell also had a strained relationship with Phil Woolpert, the USF coach. Russell respected him as a man, but he never felt that Woolpert fully appreciated him as a player, even with his dominance of the college game.

"I didn't really blame him," Russell said. "He was a good coach who had some success with his approach, but he couldn't shake his preconceived notions about how the game should be played. That was typical then. Plus, no one had ever seen my unorthodox style before, so no one knew what it was. I had to dismiss his method from my mind and find ways to develop myself on my own."

Like Cousy, he also had been an improbable basketball star, being cut in tryouts from his junior high school team in Oakland and barely making the junior varsity team as a high school sophomore. Even then he was so lightly regarded that he had to share a uniform with a teammate. He didn't start on his high school team until his senior year, and the University of San Francisco was the only team that offered him a scholarship, even that requiring a certain good fortune.

Actually, there were two instances of such fortune, both of which changed Russell's life.

The first happened when his high school jayvee coach, Bill Powles, not only kept him on the team, but also gave him two dollars so he could join the local Boys Club and have a place to develop his game.

"By that one gesture, I believe that man saved me from becoming a juvenile delinquent," he once wrote. "If I hadn't had basketball, all of my energies and frustrations would surely have been carried in some other direction."

The second?

That happened when a man name Hal DeJulio, who once had played at the University of San Francisco and now was a sort of unofficial scout for the school, had gone to a McClymonds game to scout one of Russell's teammates. Then he saw Russell. He was only a little more than six foot five then, all arms and legs. In basketball terms, he was green as new-mown grass, having few skills and no real sense of how to play. But he could run and he could jump, and he had a body that looked as if it was only going to get bigger and stronger. There was something about the young Russell that intrigued DeJulio, as if he had caught just a glimpse of the future. As fate would have it, Russell scored 14 points in that game, his career high. DeJulio arranged for Russell to get a scholarship.

"I was dumbfounded, ecstatic," Russell said. "High school was over for me with that game. As a split-session student, I was graduating. McClymonds went on to win the city championship, and I went off on a trip through British Columbia and the Northwest with a schoolboy All-Star team. I went off with a college scholarship in my pocket. Next September, I would be in college, not in a foundry."

The University of San Francisco was a small Jesuit school on the outskirts of Golden State Park. It had won the National Invitation Tournament, but it had never been known as a basketball school, not in any national sense. Most of the players were from the Bay Area. Like Holy Cross when Cousy had gone there in '47,

USF didn't even have its own gym. Playing all over the city, the team was referred to in the local papers as the "Homeless Dons." When Russell got to USF, there were only nine black students on the campus. Five were on the basketball team. One was K. C. Jones, who was from San Francisco and didn't say a whole lot. He and Russell were roommates, and even then Russell was different, a loner.

"He chose you, you didn't choose him," Jones once said.

It was a team coached by Phil Woolpert, a thin man who wore glasses and who appears almost bookish in photographs. He had been raised by liberal parents, with lessons he always remembered. He started three black players in a time when this was rarely done. So when he was criticized by some alumni for having a basketball team that did not represent the racial makeup of the campus, he shot back, "Anyone who claims that there should be discrimination toward a Negro or a Protestant or a bricklayer's son on an athletic team or in a classroom is not representative of this school, either."

Russell was six foot five when he entered USF in the fall of '53. He was six foot nine a year later. That was also the year he decided he was going to become a great basketball player, even though he knew he wasn't a great scorer. The epiphany happened at halftime in a game in Provo, Utah. He had been challenged by Woolpert and went out and played in the second half with a fury he hadn't played with before, as though he had finally found a way to channel all his anger into the game.

He already had discovered that defense was going to be his forte. He had learned that on the barnstorming tour he had taken through northern California and British Columbia in the spring of his senior year in high school, the time he had jumped up for a rebound and found himself staring at the rim, higher in the air than anyone else.

Are there little moments that give a glimpse of the possibilities?

Are there little moments that give one a glimpse of maybe a different world?

If there are, that was one such little moment for Russell.

Since then, he already had brought his questioning, analytical mind to how he could be the most effective on a basketball court. He had realized that his length and his great jumping ability were his two strengths, and he would do everything he could to utilize them as best he could. So, in a sense, he not only invented himself as a player; he also invented a personal style in which he could be successful, as unorthodox as it seemed at the time.

But along with all the wins and all the titles and all the awards and the dream life that had become his real life, there also was his evolution as a young black man in an America on the brink of change.

"My extended time there was the first I had ever spent in a virtual all-white atmosphere," he also would later write about the University of San Francisco. "There were a lot of students from small towns dotting the San Joaquin Valley who brought their religions and cultures and prejudices with them. Many of them had never interacted with black people before, and some were afraid of us for whatever reasons. Sometimes that fear erupted into confrontations. Similar encounters had accumulated since my childhood, and by the time I arrived at college they had taken their toll on my patience. To be blunt, at twenty-one I had become a psychologically aggressive person who wouldn't take crap from anyone. Keep Out. Danger zone."

These were the lessons he brought with him to Boston in

December '56. And he had arrived not just as a young basketball player about to try and find his way in a new city and a new league, not just as the only nonwhite player on the team, but as a young, educated black man in an America about to change. He also arrived with a certain attitude, one that far transcended whether he signed autographs or not.

A year later he would say in a *Sports Illustrated* article, "I don't like white people because they are white. Conversely, I like most Negroes because they are black. Show me the most downtrodden Negro, and I will say to you that he is my brother."

Later, he would say these remarks were said emotionally, that he really didn't believe them; yet he never would retract them, either, for that was never his style. He would live with his public statements, one way or the other.

"I wrote some controversial articles," he would later say, "but I believed them at the time. I was talking human rights before it was popular."

One who initially did not like Russell was broadcaster Johnny Most, who was in his fourth year as the Celtics' broadcaster and all but bled Celtics green. Already he had turned being a homer into an art form. He was closer to some of the Celtics than he was with others, but he loved all of them.

Except Russell.

"He was the first Celtic player I ever disliked," Most would later write.

Most thought Russell was cocky, arrogant, at times even hostile. Sometimes he would try to talk to him and Russell wouldn't even respond. The Garden crowd would cheer him and he wouldn't even acknowledge it. To Most, Russell and Heinsohn were complete opposites.

"Even the ushers didn't like him, often demanded he'd show his ID before they let him into the building. He thought they were peons and that he owned the damn building."

Heinsohn kept telling Most that Russell would grow on him. But it took four years, and not without Most approaching Russell.

"Bill, is there something bothering you about me?" Most asked.

"No, there's not," Russell replied. "It's nothing personal. My problems are about issues no white man would understand."

"Hey, just wait a fuckin' minute," Most countered. "That's not true. You don't know me as a person, and you have no right to judge me."

Most told him about the time he'd tried to get work on a regional college football game and was told no because he was Jewish. After that, Russell treated him differently.

But there was no understanding Russell in April 1957; not really.

It would take almost half a century and four of his books to even begin to attempt to understand William Felton Russell.

Heinsohn would later say his understanding of Russell would change as he learned more and more of the baggage he had brought with him to Boston, but in the beginning, "Buddy, buddy, we were not.

"I recognized he had problems that probably were not going to be able to be worked out," he wrote in his 1980 book.

At one point early in the play-offs, the Celtics were in the locker room when Heinsohn got a letter saying he had been named the league's rookie of the year, complete with a check for $300.

"You should give me half," said Russell, who was sitting nearby.
"Why's that?" Heinsohn asked.

"Because if I was here all year I would have gotten it," Russell said.

Later, Loscutoff would think Russell had resented Heinsohn in that season because Heinsohn was the hometown boy and had been named rookie of the year, though none of that ever came through on the court.

There's little question that Auerbach understood Russell in ways few others did. Certainly, he had understood the best way to integrate Russell into the Celtics and how to make his arrival into the NBA as easy as it could have been.

"Right from the beginning I think Russell felt at ease in my presence and with our ball club," Auerbach said. "Nobody catered to him. I simply told him what I expected him to do. Some things just can't be taught. Little by little as the days went by I began to detect this fierce pride Russell had, this incredible urge to win. I never once saw him looking at the stat sheet to see how many rebounds or assists he got. All he cared about was winning the games and, baby, that's what the name of the game is. You tell a man that and you hope he understands and appreciates what you're saying. But no one had to tell Russell what it was all about. He came to win."

Yet Auerbach slights his own role in this, too.

From the moment Russell arrived, Auerbach provided a psychological comfort zone for Russell, one that ultimately would be so effective.

How did he do this?

He told Russell he didn't care if he scored, that he essentially would count his rebounds as points. He essentially told him to just do what he felt comfortable doing on a basketball court and forget about everything else.

He had done that shortly before Russell's first game, a nationally televised one in the Boston Garden.

"I heard you can't shoot," Auerbach said. "You worried about shooting?"

"Not much," Russell answered, "but it's been on my mind."

"Well, tell you what," Auerbach countered. "Let's make a deal today, right now. When we talk contract down the line, I will never discuss statistics. All I'll discuss is if we won and how you played. That's all I care about. Don't worry about being a big scorer—I don't give a damn about that. All I want you to do is what you've always done. Play your game. And I won't tell you how to do that. Just play the way you know how."

In retrospect, this was not the easiest thing to do. Here was Russell, after all, the most celebrated college player in the country, the reason why the University of San Francisco had won fifty-five straight games and back-to-back NCAA titles, someone for whom the Celtics had traded a certified star in Macauley, and here was Auerbach telling Russell that he didn't care if he scored or not, even though scoring was the way most people judged a player's worth.

Did Auerbach do this because he wanted to take pressure off Russell?

Did he do it because he knew the Celtics really didn't need him to score?

Was it a little of both?

Regardless of the reason, though, it was a stroke of coaching genius. Not only did it instantly make Russell relax; it was the start of the incredible relationship that would develop between this Jewish coach and this young black man who didn't trust white people, this relationship that would be immortalized forever in the 2009 book *Red and Me*.

"It surprised me," Russell later said about that conversation. "The past three and a half years, no other coach had showed me such wisdom or consideration. It also left an impression because coaches back then never talked so candidly to their players. This demonstrated a giant leap of faith in me."

The other thing Auerbach did that made a distinct impression on Russell happened in his third game when he was called for goaltending on a particular play. Auerbach immediately ran out on the floor to complain about the call, a symbolic move that showed Russell his coach supported him and would fight for him.

It didn't take long for the Celtics to realize what they had in Russell, even if many in the basketball world weren't yet aware of it. In his first game, in the Garden against the Hawks on national television, he had played only twenty-one minutes; yet he still had 16 rebounds and blocked several shots, even if blocked shots were not listed in those days. They were not listed in statistics back then for the simple reason that the conventional wisdom of the time said that players leaving their feet on defense was basketball heresy.

But it hadn't been a debut out of a storybook. He had been surprised by the roughness of the game, by several of the Hawks having no qualms about putting an elbow on him, in ways that hadn't happened in the college game. He had no faith in his shooting ability, and he tired quickly. In his first couple of games he seemed tentative, unsure, a stranger in a strange land. This was not surprising since he had missed training camp and the exhibition games. It was as though he had been parachuted into the middle of an NBA season, to sink or swim, as celebrated a rookie as had ever entered the league.

Was it any wonder he felt so alone, as if he were on a private island?

It was in his fourth game, though, that the Celtics knew they were seeing something different, something they hadn't seen before.

One of the leading scorers in the league was Neil Johnston of the Philadelphia Warriors. He was a prototype NBA big man of the era, big, slow, white, relatively immobile; yet he had one great weapon—a hook shot that he could get off against anyone, and which he seldom missed. He made enough of them to go along with his line-drive jumper that he was the leading scorer in the NBA.

And then his world changed.

Russell blocked his hook shot.

Then he blocked another.

The second time he played against Johnston, Russell held him scoreless for forty-two minutes.

After that game, Eddie Gottlieb, the diminutive Philadelphia owner, and another man Damon Runyon could have created, accused Russell of playing a one-man zone, illegal under the rules. He had been one of the league's patriarchs, another man whose roots went back to the touring teams and fighting for survival. He had founded a team in Philadelphia called the SPHAs, letters that stood for the South Philadelphia Hebrew Athletic Association. The players wore Hebrew letters on the front of their shirts. They used to travel throughout the Northeast, and the word was that Gottlieb was known to stand at the hotel desk in the morning and charge his players for their phone calls the night before. Like Kerner, he believed in using entertainers as a lure to bring fans to professional basketball, and he was known for giving comedian Joey Bishop his first job.

He had begun as a promoter, everything from the House of David and the Zulu Jungle Giants baseball teams, to anything that might make people buy tickets. He also was on record opposing the NBA's integration, thinking it was economic suicide, even though in two years he would bring Wilt Chamberlain home to his native Philadelphia. Yet the issue of race would hover over the NBA well into the future. Nine years later, John Devaney of *Sport* magazine would write an article titled "Pro Basketball's Hidden Fear: Too Many Negroes in the NBA." The question asked was whether this was a justifiable fear on the owners' part, the unofficial phrase being that they all depended on "white dollars" at the gate.

And now Gottlieb was saying Russell was playing a one-man illegal zone.

Schayes had said the same thing in the Nats series with the Celtics, though he had couched it differently. He called Russell a wonderful basketball player, someone you always had to be aware of when you were driving to the basket, someone who played defense differently than any other center in the league, not someone who followed his man wherever he went, like everyone else did. He was really saying there was no question Russell was playing a zone.

But it was more than that.

It was the sense that Russell's amazing shot-blocking ability, something never seen before in the NBA, was changing things.

"Russell made shot-blocking an art," Auerbach would later say.

He would pop the ball straight up and grab it like a rebound, or else redirect it right into the hands of one of his teammates and we'd be off and running on the fast break. You never saw Russell bat a ball into the third balcony the way those other guys did. Sure, it looks powerful and the crowd goes nuts, but all it's doing is interrupting play. When Russell blocked a shot, he not only took the potential basket away from the other team, but he almost always kept the ball for his own team.

He began instilling fear into the hearts of the other players. I mean that. He didn't react normally, and as a result, no one could predict what he was going to do, which bothered the hell out of everyone. When other big men anticipated blocking a shot, the other players could sense it, so they'd come off a screen, and pump or double-pump, to upset the blocker's timing. But Russell never fell for that pump shit. He wouldn't even make a move. He'd just stand there and let the shooter make the move. Talk about intimidation. He bothered them without even moving.

That had been the beginning, the realization that this rookie was doing things in the NBA that had never been done before, even if it wasn't always easy to compute. Cousy saw it in the first game. He had been told the Celtics had gotten a player who could rebound for them, the one thing they had needed the most. But no one had ever said anything about the blocked shots, or playing the kind of defense that was going to change basketball. Cousy also had never really respected the great centers of the era, even

Mikan, as effective as he was. To him, they were all clumsy, Frankenstein types.

Not Russell.

Still, there were people who weren't sure of Russell's ability, for he wasn't like anyone else. He didn't seem particularly skilled offensively. He didn't shoot free throws very well. He only seemed to score on dunks, which were viewed differently back then, dismissed as shots that took no ability, simply height.

"Russell was the first player who dunked regularly," said the Hawks' Slater Martin, "and he did it with little flamboyance. He got it, dunked it, no big deal, and we accepted that because it was Bill's shot. We didn't consider the dunk a skilled shot. So you could jump high and you could throw the ball through the rim. So what?"

Russell already had said his favorite shot was to jump over the rim and simply place the ball in the basket.

Yet he was in the midst of changing basketball, even if few people were aware of it that first season. Yes, he was six foot ten, but there had always been large players in the NBA. What made Russell so unique was that he was a six-foot-ten athlete who could touch the top of the backboard and who also believed he could beat most NBA players in a footrace. He was a combination of both size and athleticism the game had never seen before. He loved to jump and first knew his world had changed in a high school game when one day he jumped up and found himself looking down at the basket. He had high-jumped six feet nine inches in college, one of the best performances in the country, and that had come with virtually no training, just raw athletic ability. He could touch the top of the backboard. He was agile, seemingly able to go from one side of the basket to the other with just a step or two. He wasn't just some big guy going after a rebound. He was a big guy who was a great athlete going after a rebound.

He also was the first player to turn defense into an art form, using his shot-blocking ability as both intimidation and as a weapon. He had learned in college not just to play his man, but to use his quickness and agility to almost play a one-man zone, constantly picking up opponents who had beaten their men and were headed to the basket for apparent layups before Russell seemingly would come out of nowhere to block it. This was what he had done to Heinsohn when they had played against each other the year before in Madison Square Garden, blocking five of Heinsohn's shots even though he hadn't been matched up against him, a display of athleticism Heinsohn had never seen before in a player that size.

It also changed the way the Celtics played defense, for now they always had one huge safety net behind them. Get beat by your man and yell to Russell for help. Some called it the "Hey, Bill defense." Whatever it was, it had changed the Celtics.

To see Russell play in the winter of '57 was like looking into basketball's crystal ball and seeing the game's future, however impossible that was at the time. There was no question he was an instant phenomenon, boosting crowds wherever he went, a curiosity factor if nothing else; yet it wasn't as if he had been unanimously proclaimed the game's next superstar. His game was too idiosyncratic for that, especially for fans who equated offense with basketball brilliance. To look at Russell then all but required a new way of looking at the game. Even Russell's father, in Boston with his wife to see his son play against Syracuse in the play-offs, lavished praise on Cousy at the weekly basketball luncheon he attended after his first time seeing him play as a pro.

"I heard and read a lot about Bob Cousy," the elder Russell told the crowd, "but somehow I found it hard to believe. He just couldn't be that good. Well, I saw him play Thursday night and Sunday afternoon at your Garden. What he did was hard to believe. I keep saying to myself it isn't so. But it had to be. I saw it."

Then again, Cousy's uniqueness all but jumped at people. Russell's was subtle, outside of his size and his race. He would miss two free throws and people would shake their heads, as if to say, "See, I told you he was overrated." He would occasionally take a funny-looking jump shot, as if there were too many parts and few of them were in harmony, and sportswriters would wonder just how good this guy was, anyway. He would make an offensive move that almost looked uncoordinated and after which someone would invariably ask, his voice laced with sarcasm, "This is a superstar?"

Maybe not surprisingly, it was the players who were the first to know. The Celtics knew right away, for the simple reason that not only did he make their team better, he made them better as individual players, not only rebounding the ball and throwing a great outlet pass to Cousy that ignited the fast break, but also covering up their defensive sins. From the beginning, Cousy knew Russell made the team faster. Opposing players quickly found that things they always could do against other players they simply couldn't do against Russell. It was what Heinsohn had been trying to tell people about Russell before the big guy arrived, not that anyone had really listened. But now the guys who had to go up against him every night knew.

One was Hawks center Charlie Share, the man Auerbach had drafted instead of Cousy in 1950, even though he had never played for the Celtics, essentially getting traded in the deal that brought Sharman to the Celtics.

"I'm seeing the pro game change right in front of my eyes," Share said one night after going against Russell.

He was more prophetic than he knew.

The six-foot-eleven Share was big, strong, hulking. In many ways he had been the prototype big man of the first decade of the NBA, another big moose in the Mikan tradition. Share was infamous for setting very effective picks for the Hawks' shooters—either that, or putting a big elbow in the chest of opposing centers, making them virtually unable to move. But looking at Russell and the way he could move, he realized that compared to him, he was almost inert.

"That's an awful big man," Russell had said of Share before the series started. "Real big, and he uses his weight. He'll be blocking me out under that basket."

But it was the Shares of the world Russell was so effective against, all those big immobile centers who had no answers for his quickness, his agility, his athleticism. The recognition didn't come overnight, though. Macauley would say it took the Hawks until the NBA Finals to truly know how great Russell was. For many, it would be years later, as the titles grew, as the players seemed to come and go around him; yet somehow, some way, Russell's teams always seemed to win.

Share, ultimately, would turn out to be a prophet.

So would Kerner, who said, "In big games there was no one better. In the fourth quarter he'd get every defensive rebound. How were you supposed to win when you only got one shot?"

But you didn't have to know anything about basketball to know he could run and do the kind of athletic things that smaller players could do. You didn't have to know anything about basketball to know that he was so different athletically than the other big men he was playing against, all those big slow white guys who often seemed unable to jump. You didn't have to know anything about basketball to know that when you watched him play, you were watching something different, even if maybe you weren't real sure what it was.

CHAPTER EIGHT

The Celtics were supposed to have easily taken care of the Hawks.

They were the best team in basketball, just about everyone said so.

They had finished with the best regular season record in the NBA at 44–18 and had dismissed the veteran Syracuse Nationals in three straight games to advance to the Finals.

But here they were on April 13, 1957, tied at three games apiece.

So what had happened?

What had happened was that the Hawks had turned out to be a very good basketball team, even if they hadn't started the season that way.

They had begun the season a disappointing 14–19. The coach was Red Holzman, fifteen years before he would win two NBA titles with the Knicks and find his basketball immortality in Madison Square Garden. But in the '56–57 season, he was just another young coach trying to hang on to his job. At one point, so concerned for his plight, he showed a picture of his wife and young family to his team, telling them that if the team didn't start to turn things around, he was going to get fired and wouldn't be able to take care of them.

Then he got fired.

The Hawks had been underachieving, and underachieving was something for which Kerner didn't have a lot of patience.

Kerner was thirty-nine, and he had been in professional basketball since the forties when he owned a team called the Bisons in his native Buffalo. He had made his money in game programs and concessions, and like many of the professional basketball owners then, he was both a hustler and a one-man operation. In many ways Kerner and Auerbach were similar. They were both Jewish, both headstrong, both shaped by the Depression, both intent on doing things their way. So perhaps it was inevitable they eventually would clash. Kerner also soon realized that the Tri-Cities weren't exactly major-league. So in 1951 he moved his team to Milwaukee, where his new home was an eleven-thousand-seat arena, and renamed them the Milwaukee Hawks. He might as well have stayed in the Tri-Cities.

"We wheeled and dealed and hustled to draw 366 people on opening night, and after that it fell off," Kerner would tell *Sports Illustrated* in 1960.

He ran an ad in the local papers: "Wanted. Basketball fans. No experience necessary."

He tried everything in Milwaukee, but nothing worked. He was there for four years, and every year the Hawks finished last in the Midwest Division. What was worse was that nobody came to the games. The Braves had moved to Milwaukee from Boston in

1953, and the city was crazy over baseball and the Braves, a team that quickly had captured the city's heart.

Professional basketball?

"I could crawl on my knees and I couldn't get three lines in the paper," Kerner said. "They didn't know if we were playing in the Municipal League, or on wheelchairs."

The joke was that the worst three weeks in show business were Holy Week, Christmas Week, and a week in Milwaukee. So in 1955 he moved his Hawks to St. Louis, even though professional basketball had failed there four years earlier, and the word was that, except for the Cardinals, the city was barren ground for professional sports. He was $165,000 in debt, lived with his mother, had never drawn a salary, and had never taken a day off. The rumor was he didn't have enough money to buy shoelaces for his players. But he had an irrepressible spirit, and he liked to say that when he went to bed at night, he couldn't wait for tomorrow to start.

"I came to St. Louis on a gamble," he said. "There was no other place to go. They said, 'What's his angle?' My angle? I'm trying to stay alive."

St. Louis was a great baseball town when the Hawks first arrived, with a baseball tradition that went back to 1892, when the St. Louis Browns joined the National League. Seven years later, the Browns became something called the Perfectos. When a local sportswriter heard a local woman say about their red-striped stockings and red uniforms, "What a lovely shade of cardinal," he used the new nickname in the paper; years later they became officially known as the St. Louis Cardinals. In 1926 they won their first world championship, beating Babe Ruth and the Yankees behind the greatness of player-manager Rogers Hornsby.

When the Hawks came to town, the Cardinals' star was Stan Musial, one of the best players in all of baseball. In 1954 August Busch, who owned Anheuser-Busch, one of the biggest breweries in the country, bought the team. But pro basketball already had died there, the St. Louis Bombers bombing out of business in 1951, and the St. Louis Browns had moved to Baltimore to become the Orioles. The word was that St. Louis was a lousy sports town—unless you were the Cardinals.

It also was, in many ways, a segregated town then.

Missouri had been a border state that permitted slavery, to the point that in the 1850s, both free blacks and slaves had walked the same streets. Even free blacks at that time were subjected to curfews, bans on education, and housing restrictions. Missouri law even banned blacks from learning how to read and write, the theory being that an educated black population was potentially a rebellious one. Black immigration to St. Louis increased in the early part of the twentieth century, lured by factory jobs, but there had been a significant race riot in 1917, and even by the mid-fifties, the St. Louis schools remained segregated, as were restaurants, theaters, drinking fountains, and public transportation.

But the St. Louis of the fifties was a prosperous business community. It was the second-largest trucking center in the country, a hub of the nation's grain markets, and second in the country in automobile production. Chevrolet's Corvette, the flashy sports car that had helped define the fifties, had begun to be built in St. Louis in 1954. It also was a city with an optimistic spirit, and almost from the beginning St. Louis liked the Hawks.

The Hawks' first game had been in Kiel Auditorium on November 5, 1955. The building had been built for five million and named for a former mayor. It was a magnificent structure that the Hawks players liked from the beginning, as it gave them the sense they were playing on a stage. The game program cost $.25, and the inside cover was a full-page ad for the Wabash Railroad, complete with pictures of Pettit and three other players.

WHEN THE HAWKS ARE ON THE GO, the headline said, a reminder that most of the NBA teams then did a lot of traveling by train.

Kerner was tireless.

He had found the secret to the NBA, which was promotion, and more promotion. He had a combination general manager and publicist in a young Marty Blake, who would later go on to be the NBA's longtime director of scouting, and they would do just about anything to lure fans into Kiel Auditorium and make money. Blake was another guy right out of *Guys and Dolls*, with his wild, outlandish clothes and his cigars that once were referred to as being as big as telephone poles. One thing that worked in attracting fans was to have concerts featuring such performers as Count Basie and Al Hirt, Guy Lombardo and Stan Kenton, and a guy named Paul Hahn, who did trick golf shots and hit Wiffle balls into the crowd. For the entire 1956–57 season, Kerner hired the famous clown Emmett Kelly to perform at Sunday night games.

The strategy was to make a night at Kiel Auditorium for a Hawks game an event, complete with the stylish women and suited men in the front row, as if they were at the opera, not a professional basketball game where Red Auerbach was invariably going to yell and scream at the refs. Tickets were $3.50 for seats on the floor and $1.50 for the upper deck.

"Or up with the geese," as Blake referred to them.

Another strategic ploy was to have innumerable exhibition games in the South before the season started, similar to what the Celtics did in New England. The Hawks would play here, there, and everywhere. It was all part of staying alive, the difference between making it and not making it. This was the same kind of ploy as playing an exhibition game in some draft pick's town, then cutting him the next day.

Kerner also hired a man named Buddy Blattner to be the team's broadcaster. He was the Hawks' version of Johnny Most, and he made it no secret that he, too, was a homer.

If Most had his pet names for the Celtics, Blattner had his nicknames, too. Pettit was "Big Blue," so named because he used to wear a long blue coat that had been a gift from Kerner. Slater Martin was "the Tornado from Texas." One of the reserves, Med Park, who had played at the University of Missouri, was "the Bulldog from Missouri." Hannum was "Sergeant York," named after the legendary war hero. Blattner was from St. Louis and had played a few years in the major leagues, and he unabashedly loved the Hawks.

He also had his own language:

"Bingo, it's good."

Or "They're walking the right way," after a foul was called on the opponents, sending a Hawk to the free throw line.

Kerner was his own show, too.

He also sat in the front row, across from the benches, surrounded by a group of friends, and his elderly mother who yelled at the refs with a Yiddish accent. They were called "Murderers Row," and Kerner was forever shouting, standing and waving his arms, knocking over chairs, spilling sodas on people near him, wringing his program, all the while his friends screaming at the refs in ways he couldn't—or at least in ways he shouldn't have.

"I'm the owner and I'm screaming at the refs," he once said.

"It's stupid. It's like if I opened a restaurant, and then ran outside and told people, 'Don't come in, the food stinks.' That's what I do every night, but I can't control myself."

Years later, he would say that games at Kiel were like walking into a dream. But he never forgot those early years, the ones where it was all done on a wing and a prayer.

"The best franchise is the one that makes the most money, not the one that wins the most games," he said. "That's all these things revolve around. You can only exist if you sell tickets. Nothing else."

He also had no illusions.

"Today, I'm a national figure," he would say a few years later when it was apparent the Hawks were going to make it in St. Louis. "I could have been a national bum. I call myself 'Benny the Boob.' I camouflage myself. I fight with referees, fire coaches, tear programs. You sell yourself as a character, you get space. Jack Benny changes his act. Gleason changes his. Not Kerner. I got Kernerisms."

All this had been said in a voice that was loud and emphatic one minute, almost a whisper the next. He would laugh triumphantly one minute, all but whine the next. Most of all, he was a character. He was so devoted to his mother that he promised her he would not marry until she died, a promise he kept, marrying his secretary eleven years later, after his mother's death.

And he wanted to win.

So when he bounced Holzman in early January '57, he offered the job to Pettit, his star, figuring Pettit could be a player-coach.

Pettit said no thanks.

Then he offered it to Charlie Share.

Share also said no thanks.

So Kerner turned to veteran guard Slater Martin, who had played on the great Lakers teams with Mikan.

Martin didn't want to do it.

He was the only true ball handler the Hawks had, having always felt underappreciated with the Lakers, and the last thing he wanted to do was to have to coach his teammates in addition to playing. But Kerner was the boss and he was now desperate, so Martin became the coach. From the beginning, Martin relied on Hannum, a burly forward who rarely played, to help him. Martin would come back to the bench during time-outs, and Hannum told him what was going on and what they should do about it. After a few games, Martin went back to Kerner and said that since Hannum was actually coaching the team anyway, why not give him the title? At first, Kerner refused. He never had a lot of respect for coaches in the first place; he was too much obsessed with having control of everything to like giving over his team to someone else. This was why Kerner had clashed with Auerbach back in the Tri-Cities. Plus, Kerner didn't particularly like Hannum. The feeling was reciprocal. Hannum believed Kerner saw him as just another piece of meat at the end of the bench, a guy who was all but done as a player, so why should he be paying him? But Martin kept persisting, and Kerner eventually agreed.

Hannum was from Los Angeles and had played at USC on the same team with Sharman for two years, coming into professional basketball as a six-foot-seven forward with the Indianapolis Jets in the old Basketball Association of America in 1948. By the time he got to the Hawks, he was just trying to hang in the league, so falling into the Hawks' coaching job would turn out to be a godsend. He eventually would become one of only three men in history to win NBA championships with two different teams, the other two being Pat Riley and Phil Jackson. Hannum would go on to coach six other professional teams and end up in the Hall of Fame. But all of that was far in the future when he became the Hawks' coach almost by accident.

Hannum was only thirty-one, but he had a presence. Hard-nosed, tough, and a great competitor, he took to coaching from the beginning. Macauley said Hannum was "a man's man," giving the impression that if two men had a beef, he wouldn't mind their going into a room and having only one of them walk out. His teammates called him "Old Iron Head," and he loved to pound beers after games.

"Alex was a very good coach," said Macauley. "He didn't have a whole lot of plays or anything like that, but he was a hard-nosed guy who expected everyone to play hard all the time. He expected his teachings to be followed, which was to pass the ball, move the ball, play defense, hit the open man, and, of course, get the ball to the superstar Bob Pettit."

Certainly the team responded to him, finishing 34–38, even with Pettit being out for a month with a broken wrist. In a Midwest Division where three of the four teams made the play-offs, that was enough. Then they beat both Fort Wayne and Minneapolis to advance to the Finals.

And when they upset the Celtics in the first game in the Garden in double overtime, the Celtics quickly learned that their first NBA Finals were more than just a coronation.

CHAPTER NINE

ettit had scored 37 in the first game of the Finals, a reaffirmation of his greatness.

He was another basketball success story, Cinderella in sneakers. Like Cousy, he, too, had been cut from his high school team, twice in fact. That had been in Baton Rouge, where he grew up Robert E. Lee Pettit, the son of a sheriff. He was tall in high school, but it wasn't until his last two years, when his coordination began to catch up with his size, that he blossomed into a big-time college prospect, someone who could score both inside and out. He stayed home and went to LSU, where he grew to six foot nine and became one of the best college players in the country. Maybe it was because he once had had to work hard to make his high school team, but, whatever the reason, he was always trying to get better, even as his success grew. Later he would say that he never had been satisfied, that every time he reached a goal, he made a new one for himself and set out to reach it.

In that sense, he was like many men in the fifties, the ones who had bought into America's optimism, the sense that nothing was impossible in a country that had overcome Fascism and was the most powerful country in the world. The next year he began extensive weight training, something that few basketball players ever did back then.

He had been rookie of the year in 1955, averaging 20 a game, even though there had been a lot of doubts that at only two hundred pounds he was anywhere near strong enough to survive in the bruising world of the NBA. In the next year, the Hawks' first in St. Louis, he was the league's MVP. He didn't dribble very well, but he could shoot, he could rebound, and he was extremely tenacious, one of the most respected players in the game. Russell would later say no one had more second effort than Pettit. He would go on to become one of the all-time great forwards in NBA history, but from the beginning he was a big-time scorer in the NBA, and he quickly became revered in St. Louis.

"Boy, did St. Louis love a winner," Blattner would say years later. "They talked about the Hawks in the bars and barbershops. They'd talk with great pride about 'their Hawks.'

"They weren't guys making a million dollars a year. They were guys who played their hearts out as working-class people. Many of the fans who came to the games at Kiel made more money than the players. The players didn't drive Mercedes. Many drove old Chevrolets. Their salaries were shamefully low."

Pettit and Macauley gave the Hawks two big men who could score both inside and out, and the six-foot-eleven Share, who had played in college at Bowling Green, gave them a huge front line.

They also had Hagan, the throw-in in the Russell deal, who had been a teammate of the Celtics' Ramsey at Kentucky. Both had been coached by Adolph Rupp, the so-called Baron of the Blue-grass, and the architect of the Kentucky basketball tradition that exists to this day. As a sophomore in 1951, Hagan helped Kentucky win the national title. But three players on that team had been found guilty of point-shaving, and one of Kentucky's penalties was to forfeit the '53 season, the one that would have been senior year for Hagan and Ramsey.

Both decided to come back for their senior year of eligibility the next season even though they already had graduated and had been selected in the NBA Draft by the Celtics. Ramsey had been selected in the first round, Hagan in the third, and teammate Lou Tsioropolous, who had grown up outside of Boston in Lynn, had been taken in the sixth round. Kentucky finished the season un-defeated and ranked number one in the country, but NCAA rules at the time prohibited graduate students from playing postseason games, and Kentucky declined their invitation to play in the NCAA Tournament.

So Ramsey and Hagan were linked together, as they had been since their days as Kentucky high school stars when Ramsey's Madisonville team had lost in the state finals to Hagan's Owens-boro team. Now they were playing against each other in the NBA Finals.

Hagan had been a forward in college, but six foot four was considered small to be a forward in the NBA then, so the Hawks attempted to convert him to guard, a switch that hadn't worked. But when Hannum began starting him instead of hometown fa-vorite Macauley at forward, a gutsy move, Hagan's career took off and the Hawks' season did, too.

It had only been the Hawks' second season in St. Louis, and

when they upset the Minneapolis Lakers in the Western Division Championship to advance to the NBA Finals, the *St. Louis Globe-Democrat* called it the "World Series of professional basketball."

In a sense, Frank Ramsey also revolutionized basketball.

At least the way Auerbach used him did.

Ramsey, too, could always score. He had finished his college career as the fourth all-time scorer in NCAA history, just 3 points more than Hagan. He was six foot three, another college forward who entered the NBA twixt and between positions. And in joining the Celtics, he joined a team that had Cousy and Sharman in the backcourt. What to do with him?

Enter Auerbach's ingenuity again, his ability to be creative.

One of his great strengths as a coach was never dwelling too much on players' weaknesses. Auerbach liked winners, guys who had played on great teams, had known success, knew how to fit in. He wasn't so much interested in well-rounded players as in a well-rounded team, a few skilled players, some bruisers to protect them, guys off the bench who knew their roles and who knew how to subordinate themselves for the common good. He believed in chemistry, a word that has now become overused in sports, but one that was an article of Auerbach's faith. He wanted players whose games fit in with their teammates, players who were committed to winning more than anything else. It all went back to what he told himself when he got his first coaching job with the Washington Capitols—an unknown such as he was going to get only one shot at being a professional coach, and if he was going to blow it, it was going to be because he wasn't good enough, not because some spoiled athlete ruined it for him.

In that sense, he was ahead of his time as a coach, the traditional belief being that the more good players the better, and so what if they didn't fit with one another? Chemistry? Chemistry was just a course in high school, right? Not to Auerbach. To him, it was all about team, and in many ways he was very old-fashioned: He was the undisputed boss, and everyone had to buy into his vision, or else. The shooters shot the ball. The nonshooters did not. Instead, they focused on the things they did well, even if it was only playing defense and setting screens for the shooters. It wasn't a democracy.

"Arnold was never a very lovable person," Cousy would say years later.

It wasn't necessarily his strategic knowledge that was his greatest strength as a coach. Nor was it his game plans, or his ability to give emotional pregame speeches before big games, or the symbolic lighting up of his victory cigars—none of the things that ultimately would come to define his legend. It was that he knew talent, and how to acquire it. More important, he knew people—what made them tick; what motivated them; what they wanted. To him, that was always more important than x's and o's scribbled on a blackboard.

He also coached with the knowledge that people were different and thus had to be dealt with differently. Russell didn't like to practice hard? No problem. Russell didn't have to practice hard. Later in his career Russell hardly practiced at all; he would sit in practice drinking coffee and reading the paper, all the while making fun of his teammates. And if his teammates might not have liked it? Too bad. And if people might have thought Auerbach wasn't exerting his control as a coach? That was too bad, too. Because Auerbach knew Russell played hard in the games, and it was all about winning games, not always about imposing your will.

That was Auerbach's coaching genius, his ability to create an environment all about winning and nothing else—not whether players liked one another; not whether they liked him.

It was all about winning.

Yet within that framework he gave players tremendous freedom. Cousy could throw the ball around his back and commit conventional basketball heresy all he wanted, as long as he threw passes players could catch. Heinsohn could take his crazy running hook shot from the corner all he wanted as long as he hit a couple every once in a while.

Years later Cousy would say Auerbach coached on instinct. There were few set plays, no elaborate game plan. There was no real scouting of opponents, or set substitution patterns, none of the things that are as much a part of the contemporary NBA as dance teams and message boards. To Cousy, Auerbach was more of an organizer than a coach, someone who had to do a hundred and one other things in addition to coaching his team on the floor.

"Every once in a while he would yell and scream at us," Cousy said. "Then he'd feel guilty about it and would back off for a while. Then it would all start again."

Cousy came to believe that another one of Auerbach's great skills was he always could rekindle the flames.

"I tried not to make it boring," Auerbach later said. "I had short, lively practices. I did crazy things. Like play the five smallest guys against the five tallest guys. And I always gave them a reason to win the game they were playing that night."

And he was the boss, no question about that. It was Red's way or the highway. He loved to run guys in training camp, and if one of them threw up in the process, well that was even better. He believed most teams played themselves into shape and treated training camp as summer camp, so he was the opposite. His camps were notorious, the players forever secretly complaining, but he believed they were the reason for the Celtics' fast starts to seasons. He was forever taking his teams through the tank towns of New England during the preseason, both as a way to make some money and to develop camaraderie. He would drive one of the cars himself, often driving so fast that many of the players were afraid to go with him. Cousy even had it written it into his contract that he didn't have to ride with Auerbach. He loved training camp, away from the wives and the distractions, just him and his team, one big boys' club. The Celtics were Auerbach's show, no question about it, and he ran it like a court with no appeals. He didn't care about being liked. He didn't care about being one of the guys.

Russell wrote in one of his books that a scene in the movie *The African Queen* shows leeches fastening themselves to Humphrey Bogart while he's in the river, almost driving him crazy. He draws a parallel, explaining, "That's the way Red could get on you. And the only difference between him and the leeches was that he always lets you know how much he enjoys it."

Auerbach devised the perfect role for Ramsey. He would be the sixth man, and when he came into the game, he was to come in shooting.

He had been signed by Auerbach in the dugout at Fenway Park while the Celtics were playing an exhibition game. He was blond and spoke with an occasional stutter. He also was pigeon-toed and heavy-legged. More important, he was quicker than he looked, not with the kind of quickness that stood out on the court, but with the kind of sneaky quickness that often enabled him to get around defenders when you didn't think he would be able to. He was called "cute," not for his appearance, but for the smart way he played. A few years later he would write an article in *Sports Illustrated* describing all the artful ways he knew to draw fouls in the NBA.

This, too, endeared him to Auerbach, who essentially viewed basketball the same way, the simple premise being that it was all gamesmanship, and the overriding premise being that, Grantland Rice be damned, it wasn't how you played the game, but what the scoreboard said at the end of it. This attitude was one of the many reasons why the Boston sportswriters hadn't liked Auerbach back in the beginning, as he once essentially had told them at a weekly basketball luncheon that he was all about winning; sportsmanship should be saved for the playing fields of Eton.

The drafting of Ramsey was another example of Auerbach's shrewdness in evaluating players, a skill he later would be trumpeted for as the titles started to come and his legend grew. He had first seen Ramsey play in the Catskills, back in the days before the college scandals of the early fifties. It was a climate that would get blamed for being one of the incubators of the point-shaving scandals, the theory being that it had brought college players and gamblers together; yet it had been a place where Auerbach had seen Ramsey play, no insignificant thing in a basketball world of no college scouting and where too few NBA coaches saw many college games.

So Auerbach knew that Ramsey could shoot and that he was one of the team's best offensive players, and he put him in a role to take advantage of that. Before Ramsey, the sixth man was just another guy off the bench, someone whose entrance into the game at the expense of the starters meant the team had just gotten worse, conventional wisdom being that the best five players started the games. Auerbach put an asterisk on conventional thinking. Ramsey's job was to come in and make the Celtics, if not exactly better, then certainly different.

It was the start of the Celtics' tradition of the sixth man, a role that later would be played so expertly by both John Havlicek and Kevin McHale. The sixth man came in and changed the way the Celtics looked, the way they played. Ramsey came in to shoot the ball, to score the ball; not only was it a dose of instant offense, it also took pressure off Cousy, Sharman, and Heinsohn. Ramsey's job was to shoot, and everyone else knew it, to the point that Russell once said that when Ramsey came into the game, it was everyone else's job to help him get shots.

"Here is a player that can move into the frontcourt or backcourt and become a take-charge guy," Joe Looney wrote in the *Boston Herald* on the eve of the Celtics' first trip to St. Louis in the NBA Finals. "Most coaches would be satisfied with a replacement who could hold the line when the regulars are taking a breath, but Ramsey is the type capable of breaking the game wide open."

It was Looney's contention that Ramsey's presence gave the Celtics a stronger bench than the Hawks. He went on to say that in Ramsey's rookie year in the 1954–55 season he was a freshman star, but he had improved considerably since then, primarily because he now shot one-handed instead of two-handed. Ramsey credited Cousy with that, saying that Cousy had told him that shooting one-handed gave the shot a quicker take-off, making it easier to get off in front of an opponent.

"I practiced the one-handed shot whenever I could when I was in the service," Ramsey said. "It has paid off. It is much easier to drive, too, when you're maneuvering the ball at the start with one hand instead of two. And driving in always has been an important part of the scoring I've always done."

Ramsey was conservative, both in this nature and in his appearance. He was the personification of the fifties version of the all-American boy, as if he had stepped off the cover of the *Saturday Evening Post*. He often wore suits, and he always lined his shoes up in front of his locker. He was always thinking about money—how to acquire it; how to invest it; how to keep it from the government. He loved looking for loopholes in the tax law. He often said that his home was in Kentucky, and the only reason he was in Boston was to make money—all of this said with his native Kentucky in his speech. He also had a slight stutter, which led one night to a memorable encounter with Auerbach.

"Having trouble with your *f*'s?" Auerback asked.

"Fuck you, Red," Ramsey shot back. "How are those *f*'s?"

But Auerbach loved Ramsey, to the point that when Ramsey retired in '64, he was offered the chance to be Auerbach's assistant coach, something Auerbach never had, with the understanding that he would become the next Celtics coach when Auerbach decided to step down. Ramsey said no thanks; he was going back home to Kentucky to make real money.

To him, the play-offs were the ultimate money time, no small thing in a league where everyone worked in the off-season and where no one ever seemed to have enough money.

"You're playing for my money now," Ramsey would tell his teammates.

Cousy always said Ramsey was the most mature of all of them.

———

The Hawks' last-second win in the sixth game had come before a sellout crowd of 10,053 in Kiel Auditorium. It also had been another great game, the lead changing twenty-three times, the score tied twenty times, and each team had twice called time-outs in the last minute to set up shots.

The game had tied the series at three games apiece.

But the Celtics had been down two times in this series, losing the opening game in the Garden, and the first game in Kiel Auditorium, the game that had been preceded by the incident between Auerbach and Kerner. And just when they seemed to have taken control of the series by winning the fifth game by 15 in the Boston Garden, the Hawks had forced a seventh game, returning to the Garden, where they had already won a game and had already proved to the basketball world that they could win this series, even if the consensus going into the series had been that the Celtics were the NBA's best team.

Hadn't Dave Egan, the *Boston Record*'s acerbic columnist known as "the Colonel," the man who routinely killed Ted Williams in his widely read columns, called them "the best team in basketball history"? The *Record* was a tabloid with a circulation near five hundred thousand. Part of the great Hearst newspaper chain, it was a snapshot of all the Hearst papers, with big catchy headlines, a lot of pictures, short, punchy stories, and sports columnists who led with their attitude, the more contrarian the better.

The columnists were king, the only real voice in the wilderness, their influence powerful, and Egan was the most popular. He had gone both to Harvard and to Harvard Law School and had become, both for his writing talent and his constant attacks on

Williams, larger than life in the Boston newspaper world, a very competitive one with six newspapers. In many ways Egan was right out of *Front Page*, a hard-drinking, hard-living man infamous for spending the afternoon in a barroom, then stumbling back to the newsroom to write another great column in a tabloid with a huge circulation. Some people loved Egan. Some people hated him. Most everyone read him.

And he always had liked Auerbach, going back to those early years when most sportswriters didn't.

In fact, he had written a column, way back in 1950, defending the new coach, even comparing him to the famed football coach Frank Leahy, who had taken Boston College to the Sugar Bowl before departing for Notre Dame.

"We know now, as Syracuse, Fort Wayne and Minneapolis and the giants of the game come striding towards Boston, that a winner has been forced upon us in the person of Red Auerbach of the Celtics," Egan wrote, "and that he will do for professional basketball in this town what Frank Leahy did for intercollegiate football. . . . We know this not by anything he has said, but by the performance of his team. . . . This is not a team of ballerinas and prima donnas and temperamental selfish stars. They are young and hungry and full of heart, and they play the rambunctious, enthusiastic, blood-and-thunder basketball, which only the young and the hungry and only the hearty can play."

Auerbach would later say that Egan saved him in Boston in those early years.

Back then, though, Egan was just a lonely voice in the basketball wilderness.

Now it was different; Egan's calling the Celtics the greatest team in NBA history was huge, a reaffirmation that they could be what Walter Brown always hoped they could be, especially in those days when even his friends thought the team was his personal folly.

Now, on this morning of the seventh game, they were on the front page of the *Boston Globe*, a symbolic reminder that the Celtics were in uncharted territory, complete with a cadre of fans who had spent the night in the lobby of the Garden in hopes of getting tickets when the box office opened. Who would ever have believed that?

CHAPTER TEN

The decade of the fifties was one of transition. In the America that would come afterward, an America of civil rights, Vietnam, feminism, and the birth of the counter-culture, the country's values seemed to be under attack.

Although the seeds of that were all to be found in the fifties, it was nonetheless a hopeful decade, an optimistic one. America had defeated Fascism and made the world safe for democracy; there was nothing the United States couldn't do. It was a decade marked by the rise of the suburbs, the exodus out of the cities of people looking for a better life than their parents had, whether that meant owning their home, watching their kid play Little League, or sitting around with the family at night watching this new thing called television.

This was the American Dream, and it came into everyone's living room in weekly television shows such as *The Adventures of Ozzie and Harriet*, *Father Knows Best*, and *Leave It to Beaver*.

These programs were all remarkably similar, portraying the new, idealized American family living in a clean, well-lighted place in some generic suburb where trouble meant some kid smoking behind the school. These TV worlds had no racism, no unhappy women frustrated by doing the cooking and the cleaning, no rebellious kids chafing at the conformity they saw all around them, no unhappy families. There were no ethnics, save for Ricky Ricardo on *I Love Lucy*, which at one point was watched every week by thirty million viewers. The main characters in these popular TV shows of the fifties were distinctly American, with their Anglo-Saxon names, their understated manner, their unchallenged belief in the system. These were shows that depicted a prosperous and hopeful America, one that had come so far from the Depression and the horror of World War II.

It was a decade where people were looking to reinvent themselves, as if anything was possible in this new America, one that was changing from an agrarian country to a suburban one. There was the GI Bill for the men who had served in the armed forces. There was the exodus west to California, where as one popular song a decade later would say, "palm trees grow, rents are low, and the feeling is 'lay back.'" There was the sense that everyone could own a little piece of the good life, the sense that America was the most powerful country in the world, and to the victors belonged the spoils.

The Celtics were all examples of this, if sometimes in different ways.

They all had been to college, the first people in their family to do so. With the exception of Auerbach, they all had been young enough to have escaped the war, though Ramsey had been in the Army for a year in the aftermath of the police action in Korea.

Almost all came from working-class roots, or small towns that traditionally had offered few opportunities. All had been shaped by their college experience; all had seen their worlds expanded. Maybe most important, all believed in that most American of beliefs of the era that you could write your own script.

Why not?

Hadn't Auerbach already come so very far from the grim Brooklyn of his childhood?

Hadn't Cousy already come so very far from the tenement of his Manhattan childhood, the one where there hadn't been any running water, and the small house in St. Alban's, Queens, where there always had been too much tension and too little money?

Hadn't Russell, even with his anger and memories of old hurts, already come so far from the overt racism and limited opportunity of his father's life?

This was just one of the things these three shared, even if it wasn't articulated.

There's no doubt Cousy and Auerbach shared certain similarities, given they both had been products of the Depression, products of ethnic ghettos in New York, at least in Cousy's early years. To Cousy, the lesson learned back there in those streets that had crushed so many dreams was kill or be killed, that the only way you survived was by stepping over someone else, that it was always you against the other guy, that when you stripped sport down to its essence, that was what lay at the core.

Yet unlike many of the men who had grown up in the same era and the same circumstances, Cousy never romanticized it. He knew that no one was more competitive than he and that he had become the player he was because of that drive. Still, as he grew older, he also came to know there was a negative side to it, too.

This so-called killer instinct had to be controlled; left unchecked, it could be destructive.

He even published a book on the subject, although it would come eighteen years later, in 1975. Called *The Killer Instinct*, it was written with John Devaney. The book's cover was black with a close-up of Cousy's face, and the heading at the top said, "Mr. Basketball thought winning was the only thing—until the hunger to win as a coach drove him to the edge of moral and physical collapse."

The original idea had been an exposé of college basketball, about the abuses in the college game, but it had turned out to be more personal. He had coached at Boston College after leaving the Celtics in 1963, then later in the NBA with the Cincinnati Royals before finding himself sitting alone in a hotel room after games and drinking scotch out of a big glass. He had left his family behind in Worcester then, and he had come not only to regret that, but also to feel guilty about it, once again putting himself and his career above his family. Maybe most of all, though, the core of the book's message is captured by a scene describing a summer camp experience when he was maybe five years removed from playing for the Celtics. He had been in a camp pickup game, and he and one of his counselors, a kid who played at Colgate, had gone after a loose ball. The kid had inadvertently hit Cousy with an elbow, and as they both went to the ground for the ball, Cousy wrestled the ball away, exhibiting more force than necessary, and then hit the kid with an elbow as he started back down the court as the kid lay bleeding on the ground behind him. Moments later he felt awful, and that night sat with the kid, endlessly apologizing.

"I came out of the big-city ghetto chasing the American Dream like millions of men and women of my generation," he wrote. "It was all about survival, every man for himself. I had always wanted to be a success in everything I tried. In competition I had an almost uncontrollable need to win. That killer instinct had brought me success as a player and a coach, but it also tempted me to run over people, to break rules, to neglect my family, to neglect myself to the point of exhaustion. I am no longer proud of my killer instinct. It's something I must live with the best I can."

That would come later, of course, but even in 1957, at the height of his career, he knew the grip this had on his life, the reason why, even though he was now at his professional pinnacle, he felt more and more pressure to live up to the standards he now set for himself.

Cousy knew Auerbach had the same instincts, the same single-mindedness, the sense that he would do anything to win, even if that required living in a Copley Square hotel room in Boston while his family lived in Washington. He knew that, to Auerbach, everything—a game, a practice, a conversation, everything—was a competition.

"We both had our roots in those New York ghettos," Cousy said.

That was not a throwaway line.

Cousy knew he had been forever scarred by his childhood, and these wounds were always with him: wariness with people, his lack of trust, the sense that all these strong emotions were perpetually churning inside him, the emotions that had been fuel to his incredible drive, his constant striving for perfection, not only for himself, but for the people around him, too. He was famous for throwing the ball just a little ahead of one of his teammates if he didn't think the person was running hard enough on a fast break, or throwing the ball at the back of someone's head if the person wasn't in the proper place. He was always on Heinsohn to get in better shape, to knock off the cigarettes. He would sit by himself in hotel rooms before games and brood, retreating more and more into himself, working himself up to hate the man he would be matched up against in all those little wars across the NBA, his own little pregame hell.

He knew Auerbach had been scarred, too, and that this was the reason he never seemed able to get really close to anyone as well as the reason he always needed a certain distance, a certain control. He saw it in many ways—the way he would tell the players he wasn't married to them, the message being that if you crossed him, he would get rid of you; the way the Celtics were his team, no matter what the masthead said; the way he always lorded something over the players, be it meal money, days off, length of practices—something.

"Arnold was many things," Cousy would later say, when all the games had been played, the battles won, "but he was not a lovable man."

Cousy thought Russell was more complicated than even Auerbach, though. Cousy thought that much of Russell's competitive drive was racially motivated and came from his immense pride, as though every rebound and every blocked shot was his way of making a social statement. There were times he thought that Russell didn't even like basketball, that the game was just something he was great at, a socially acceptable vehicle for his anger. He also knew Russell would never compromise, not for a minute.

But, to Heinsohn, the three were very similar—the Jewish coach who had grown up in a Brooklyn ghetto in the midst of the

Depression; the point guard who had spent his early years in the tenement world of Manhattan, the only son of French immigrants; and the African-American who had spent his childhood in the segregated South. To him, they all shared something in their genetic makeup. They didn't just want to win. They had to win, as if winning had become a form of validation. Heinsohn called it the "love ache," his theory being that their need to win again and again was a form of love deprivation, a hunger they could never satisfy.

He quickly learned that you didn't challenge Auerbach, you didn't question him, that Auerbach simply wasn't psychologically prepared to deal with that. He believed Russell had an almost neurotic need to win, and that as much as he said he didn't care about adulation, Heinsohn always thought it was just the opposite—that he was always seeking adulation and that at some psychological level, that was the reason he played in the first place. He knew Cousy had a speech impediment and that Ramsey had a domineering father. He knew Sharman was an obsessive man who always carried vitamins in his suitcase, and that he had been the neighborhood Nazi in grammar school, the one who always had to fight his way home after school. To him, they were all driven by something, something they couldn't even articulate.

"I don't know for a fact," he once wrote years later, "but my guess is that all these guys were driven by a need for acceptance, for dramatic reassurance in their own minds of their own worth, and they found that reassurance through excellence in sport."

He knew he did.

There was little question Auerbach, Cousy, and Russell were all the ultimate overachievers, at least in light of how their basketball journeys had started out. Both Cousy and Russell had been cut from their high school teams. Auerbach had been an undistinguished college player. Not even a scriptwriter with an overwrought imagination could have dreamed up how far they would go in the game. Heinsohn might have been right—maybe there was something in their makeup that made them not only want to win, but have to win. Certainly, they all paid an emotional price, from Russell's throwing up minutes before big games, to Cousy's sleepwalking, to Auerbach's going through the world as if everyone else was the enemy, someone to parry with, overcome; this man who spent most of his life living in a hotel by himself, away from his family, while chasing his own dreams, however private.

"A man who spent the lonely nights of the season locked up in his hotel room eating Chinese food off a hotplate," Russell wrote in his first book, *Go Up for Glory.*

For years Cousy would awaken from sleep to walk around the room talking to himself, then remembering none of it the next day. Sharman said that when they roomed together all those years on the road, it was not uncommon for him to awaken in the middle of the night to see Cousy walking around the room speaking French, the language he had spoken as a young child. One year at his basketball camp in southern New Hampshire, Cousy ran out of the cabin where he'd been sleeping and ended up running down a road naked. When he eventually saw a doctor about these episodes, he was told he was having anxiety attacks and was given medication for them. By the end of his career, he would develop a nervous tic under his right eye.

Throughout all his unbelievable success, through this career he never could have envisioned, he never got over his fear of failure, the fear that somehow he would fail and be psychologically naked in front of all those people in all those arenas. Strangely, this inner fear coexisted with the extreme confidence he clearly felt and displayed on the court. It was as though there were two sides to his psychological makeup, constantly at war with each other. Later in his career, in those years before he finally retired in 1963, he only felt more pressure, as if all the accolades and all the cheers no longer mattered. He still felt he always had to prove it, that everything he had worked for could vanish in the blink of an eye. For he knew the NBA was better than it had been when he had started out in it; he knew it was becoming more difficult to excel in a basketball world where he was still considered the fastest gun in the West and all the bars in all the little Western towns were full of young guys just waiting to go out in the dusty street and slap leather with him.

"I'm thirty-four years old and I'm still a boy having to prove myself over again every time out," he would say in his last season. "But if I've spent my life playing a boy's game, it's still what I do. And because it's what I do, I want to be the best. It's not enough to be good enough. I have to be the best because that's what it's all about."

And the older he grew as a player, the more he resented the time on the road, the time away from his wife and two young daughters, the emotional price he paid for the life he had chosen, however beneficial it had been. His daughters, almost strangers to him, were growing up, and he felt guilty that his family's life always revolved around him with his games, his schedule, his life. There were times he'd be in some hotel room someplace, trying to psyche himself up for still another game, still another night when he had to be Bob Cousy once again, the player so many of the young guards coming into the league wanted to make their reputation against, and he would wonder about his life, the choices he was making.

"My daughters would grow up and get married and what would I remember?" he once said. "A thousand hotel rooms?"

The other thing he and Russell shared, even if they didn't know it in their first season together, was their ambivalence about their chosen profession. Both felt that playing basketball for a living was not what they had gone to college to do; that it might even be a questionable profession for an adult.

"One good teacher is worth the whole lot of us," Cousy often would say, calling basketball a child's game.

Russell, later in his career, would come to see basketball as almost trivial, not worthy for a grown man in a complicated world. He was almost embarrassed even to be playing it.

This sense of a social conscience was the other thing Cousy and Russell shared, even if it was rarely articulated. It was more obvious with Russell, with his political activism. He was one of the first athletes to refer to himself as "black," back when that word had become politicized. He had a propensity to speak out on racial issues in America. He also publicized his trip to Liberia, where he called Africa his ancestral home. Then again, Cousy always had been more private.

Still, even if later in his life Cousy wished he had done more for society than play basketball, he had been one of the founders of the National Basketball Players Association, he was active in several progressive causes, and he always had an acute sense of prejudice.

"The black players always liked Cousy," once said Barksdale, who had played for the Celtics in the early fifties, "because he always was very sensitive to us."

Ultimately, they were the three transformational figures in the Celtics' story, the ones who were about the NBA's future, while so many others of that era were locked firmly in a certain time and place. Cousy was the first modern point guard, the prototype for all the others who would come after him. Russell was the first African-American superstar. Auerbach arguably was the first modern NBA coach. Seen in the context of basketball history, all three were ahead of their time, brought together by basketball fate.

Auerbach later would say that Cousy and Russell were two of the four men who had changed basketball. The first had been Hank Luisetti, the Stanford all-American in the forties who had originated the jump shot. The second had been Mikan, the first great pivot scorer. Then there had been Cousy for his distinctive approach to the game and the way he ran the fast break offense, and Russell for his shot-blocking and use of defense as a weapon.

To Auerbach, these men were the game's Mount Rushmore, basketball's mountain depicting the faces of those whose legacies towered above all the others.

Yet he, too, belonged on that same very small basketball mountaintop.

What were the odds that three of them would be part of the same team at the same time?

Could there be odds that high?

Each had arrived in Boston in his own circuitous way; each benefited from the other two. Could Cousy have been Cousy on a team that walked the ball up the court, constantly looking to get the ball inside to the big men? Could he have played for a traditionalist coach who didn't like his freewheeling, idiosyncratic style? Could his emotions have dealt with being in a losing situation, a little six-foot-one guard trying to win games all by himself, the defenses always stacked against him because there was really no one else?

Could Russell have been Russell playing for a coach who wanted him to shoot and be more of a traditional center because he was paying him a lot of money and that was what guys making all the money were supposed to do? Could he have been the Russell we've come to know playing for a coach he didn't respect?

Could Auerbach have been Auerbach without Russell and Cousy, or would it always have been his fate to be just another abrasive coach yelling at referees and arguing with sportswriters, just another coach that no one ever really understood, never mind appreciated?

These are the great unanswered questions, for both fate and the basketball gods brought these three disparate men together in a special time and a special place. Cousy, Russell, and Auerbach would always be linked together in ways no one ever could have envisioned in that spring of '57, three men who always would have their big slice of basketball immortality, their reputations forever cemented, while so many others from their era would get lost, casualties of time.

Only no one knew it yet.

The mid-fifties saw the proliferation of what would become known as popular culture, complete with the birth of several things that would become American icons: McDonald's, Disneyland, *The Tonight Show*, frozen dinners, Marilyn Monroe, suburban shopping malls, Holiday Inn, Frisbee, Kentucky Fried Chicken, *Sports Illustrated*, *TV Guide*, and *Playboy*, which in 1956, just three years after its inception, had a circulation of six hundred thousand. The mid-fifties saw the birth of corporate culture and the accelerated growth of white-collar workers, the man in the gray flannel suit. It also saw the birth of the interstate highway system, the ultimate symbol that anything was possible; all you had to do was get in your car and go after it.

Most of all, it was the explosion of television that moved like a comet throughout the decade, changing advertising, changing behavior, changing popular culture, changing politics, changing everything.

Yet in all the important ways, the Celtics were the products of the underbelly of the fifties, especially Cousy, Auerbach, and Russell. It was the fifties of competition, of moving ahead, of letting nothing get in the way of your dreams. It was a decade of fighting against old prejudices, of eradicating old hurts. Certainly it was for Russell, who already had moved way beyond his father's world, someone who had used basketball not only to go to college, but as a way to make money in the white man's world that had nothing to do with being subservient. If all three certainly had benefited from the opportunities the decade provided, no doubt far surpassing their parents' lives, the traditional measuring stick for success in America, it was Russell's struggle that spoke to the changes about to come in America.

The fifties also saw the birth of rock and roll, a hybrid form of Negro rhythm and blues, which always had euphemistically been called "race music," and white country-and-western music. These were the two foundations that Elvis mined so well, with his duck-tail haircut, his "Elvis the Pelvis" nickname, and a unique style that made him a national phenomenon. As Ed Sullivan, host of the Sunday night TV staple *The Ed Sullivan Show*, so aptly described it, "I don't know what he does, but it drives people crazy."

Sullivan, who had been a gossip columnist in New York before hosting his own entertainment show, had first resisted the plan to bring Presley on his show. Sullivan was a straitlaced man, never really comfortable in front of the camera, and in the beginning he no doubt looked at Presley as if he had just arrived from some other planet. But the moment Presley first appeared, with Sullivan deciding not to film him from the waist down, the ratings went through the roof and out across the country like the speed of light. There was no turning back.

Rock 'n' roll captured a generation of young people, now being called "baby boomers" since they had been born after the war. It was a group targeted so successfully by the rising advertising business that youth culture became an economic force, one that exists to this day. It was the music that would capture a generation of young people, a music with a rebellious spirit, music that, in many ways, would be the spawning ground for the counterculture of the sixties. It had been announced to mainstream America by *Time* magazine in January 1956. The article said the music featured characteristics such as "choleric saxophone honking mating-call sounds." It then went on to alert the country that something insidious was coming out of its kids' radios in this genre of music performed by "a vocal group that shudders and exercises violently to the beat while roughly chanting either a near nonsense phrase or a moronic lyric in hillbilly idiom."

But who cared what *TIME* said?

Certainly not a new generation that couldn't wait to turn the radio up.

Youth culture had been born, complete with rock 'n' roll as its anthem.

The other significant influence on a new generation of American youth was black culture, not only in music, but in sports, something sports fans in New England certainly were seeing with Russell's arrival, even if they sometimes didn't seem aware of it. Jackie Robinson had integrated baseball just a decade before, but already he had been followed by such talented players as Willie Mays, Ernie Banks, and Henry Aaron. Three years earlier, Mays had hit 51 home runs, and seemed to routinely make plays in the outfield that seemed almost otherworldly. The best college football player in the fall of '56 had been Jim Brown of Syracuse, so good an athlete that he also starred in basketball at Syracuse and was called the best college lacrosse player in the country. And, of course, there was Russell, who along with teammate K. C. Jones, had led San Francisco to two straight NCAA Tournaments and a winning streak of fifty-five games, and now was the reason the Celtics were being called the best team in basketball.

There is no overestimating this.

To a generation of kids coming of age in the fifties, it was possible to now look at blacks differently than their parents had, and sports were a huge part of that. If nothing else, it individualized blacks, made white America look at them as people, and not just as a faceless group. It personalized them in ways that rarely had been done before in the larger culture.

It also sent out a message, subliminal as it might have been in the beginning, that the country was changing. The marches in the South appeared on the nightly news. The civil rights movement was emerging. There was the definite rise of the black athlete. All were part of the same mosaic, one that was starting to look at African-Americans in ways they hadn't been looked at before.

In just a few years such black stars as Elgin Baylor, Wilt Chamberlain, and Oscar Robertson would follow Russell to NBA superstardom, changing basketball forever. But in '57, Russell was the NBA's first black superstar, even if no one really knew then how influential he'd become. But one thing was clear: America was beginning to see the kind of athlete it had never seen before, and a generation of American youth was beginning to look at blacks in new ways.

"Clearly, a social revolution wrought by great athletes was taking place, and it was in many ways outstripping the revolution engineered by the Supreme Court of the United States and by Martin Luther King Jr., in the streets of the nation's Southern cities," wrote David Halberstam in his 1993 book *The Fifties*. "If the face of America, at its highest business, legal, and financial level, was still almost exclusively white, then the soul of America, as manifested in its music and its sports, was changing quickly."

It was a decade often now remembered as a placid one, the white-bread fifties, but there were undercurrents, too, portents of the future. *On the Road*, the novel by Jack Kerouac, the former Columbia football player who had grown up in Lowell, Massachusetts, had come out in '57. It became the anthem of the beat movement, which was rebelling against the sterile conformity of American life. One of the most popular novels of the year was Grace Metalious's *Peyton Place*, which uncovered the sexual secrets of a small New Hampshire town. Another was *Catcher in the Rye*, J. D. Salinger's searing look at a prep school boy trying to deal with the phoniness of the world he found himself in.

All three were ahead of their time, almost visionary, dealing with themes that would all but be mainstreamed a decade later. In many ways not understood at the time, the seeds of the sixties were all being sown in the fifties. From the war on Communism, to drug experimentation and disaffected youth, from the Pill and women's liberation to rebelling against the conformity of mainstream American life, the brush fires were all there in the fifties, just waiting for another decade to fan the flames.

Sports were changing, too, fueled by television that more and more seemed to be in everyone's living room, making professional sports, and the people who played them, more and more accessible. That the seventh game between the Celtics and Hawks was going to be the first NBA Final ever to be nationally televised emphatically spoke to this.

It wasn't just a great game.

It was a great game seen by a national television audience.

But the NBA was still, in all the important ways, a regional league. It didn't go west of Minneapolis. It didn't go south of St. Louis. There were only eight teams, with five of them in the Midwest. Occasionally, there would be doubleheaders in Madison Square Garden, which meant that on those nights, half the league would be in New York City. Most players were still making very little money, at least compared to baseball. Meal money on the road was five dollars.

The Celtics still played half a dozen "home games," in a drafty old arena in Providence, Rhode Island, that all but screamed out minor league. Once, a couple of years before, the Celtics had played with the floor so slippery the players were sliding on virtually every play. Visiting players in Syracuse were still routinely hit by bottle caps and pennies. The word was owner Lester Harrison of the Rochester Royals would have the water turned off in the visitor's locker room if his team lost, and that he and his brother were known to scalp tickets outside the building.

In many ways the NBA was still minor-league on the American sports scene, even though it sometimes seemed to be growing exponentially and had already come so far in the past decade.

This was why these NBA Finals were so important, both from a marketing standpoint, although no one ever used the term back then, and for how the NBA was perceived. For the attitude about basketball was changing. The college game was beginning to recover from the scandals of the early fifties, with the building of spacious new field houses at Kansas, Maryland, and Ohio State, and the fact that the NCAA Finals of just a month earlier had featured a great upset, North Carolina beating Kansas and its sophomore seven-foot-one star Wilt Chamberlain. He already was being called the game's next great player, someone who had been talked about since he was a high school player in Philadelphia. He already had been coached for a short while by Auerbach in the Catskills when Chamberlain had still been in high school, Auerbach telling him he should go to college at Harvard so the Celtics would own his rights in the territorial draft. There was the palpable sense the game was becoming more mainstream, more accepted by the sporting public.

And the Celtics were in the very forefront of that change, primarily because of Cousy and Russell.

Over time, their relationship would cool, not in any unfriendly, hostile way, but because of the realities of Boston and Cousy's fame. He was the media darling, and Russell was the six-foot-ten Negro who often seemed to have a wall around him that not only kept people away but could intimidate them, too.

Someone would come up to Russell and say, "I just shook the

hand of the best basketball player in the world, and now I want to shake the hand of the second best," the kind of remark that simply reinforced to Russell that whatever he did in Boston would never be enough.

Years later Russell would say he had tremendous respect for Cousy as both a player and a person; yet they were never friends in the real sense of the word. He would say he came to respect the pressures Cousy was under being a superstar in the NBA, and he thought Cousy respected him, too, but it wasn't as though they spent a lot of time off the court together. Years later, Cousy always said he simply had been too immersed in his own world.

It was something Auerbach picked up on, one more example of his fine-tuned antenna when it came to his team and his players. He not only knew the pressures on Russell, but he also knew that few appreciated his greatness.

"Maybe if he had been a white Holy Cross hero it would have been different," he would say years later in his autobiography.

But there was never any problem in the beginning, in that first championship season.

Cousy was at the height of his fame. Not only was he the biggest draw on the road, he was also by far the player with the most endorsements, one of the few names that transcended the NBA, someone on the cusp of becoming a true American celebrity. In this way he was like Ted Williams, Mickey Mantle, and Willie Mays; Ben Hogan and Sam Snead; or boxer Rocky Marciano.

It wasn't just the fact he'd been on the cover of *Sports Illustrated* a year earlier. It was the fact this hadn't been some basketball magazine with its limited circulation and its narrow focus, or some story on the sports page. This was a slick new magazine from one of the media giants in the country, a magazine aimed at a mass audience, one targeted for a more affluent, suburban America, an ambitious magazine, its goal being to cover the breadth of American sport in a way never done before.

It had been the first time the NBA had been on a *Sports Illustrated* cover, the message being that the NBA was no longer something merely on the periphery of American sport squeezed in between college football and the start of spring training. This was the kind of national legitimacy the NBA had never had before. There was no denying that baseball was still the undisputed king, America's pastime, a game deeply rooted in the national fabric, but in that *Sports Illustrated* article was the message that professional basketball was a sport to start paying attention to; no longer a goon's game, it was a game with its own artistry.

"Cousy has opened the road to better basketball," the magazine said, while also calling him the greatest all-around player in the sixty-four-year history of basketball.

The magazine also called Cousy a basketball visionary, saying that "from now on the new stars will play like Cousy. You can see his influence in backyards throughout the country."

CHAPTER ELEVEN

I f everyone in the game knew Cousy's significance, Russell's was harder to quantify, especially in that first year before there were any NBA titles.

Auerbach was always telling the Boston sportswriters how good he was, a missionary forever preaching the gospel, but it often fell on deaf ears, courtesy of the Boston sportswriters' collective lack of basketball knowledge, and their general dislike of Auerbach.

"Russell is going to be the best center in the business," Auerbach said. "I've never seen anyone do what he did—come in at midseason with no experience, no training, and no knowledge of the league and take right over."

Yet Russell's individual game was almost an acquired taste, something that required a knowledge of how basketball games were actually won. Looking at him was a little like looking at modern art after growing up on landscapes. Understanding and appreciating this player, this "basketball art form," required a new way of seeing the game that incorporated a different approach not reliant exclusively on offense. For too many people in Boston, if Russell didn't shoot very well, how good could he be, right? That seemed to be the consensus that first year, even to those who admitted that the addition of Russell certainly had made the Celtics better.

Still, it was not always an easy sell.

"Is Russell worth $17,000?" Worcester sportswriter Tom Carey had asked when Russell had been signed. "No, because I can name four rebounders Russell fears. In plain basketball terms, he's a vastly overrated competitor. He has ailments, too. Too tired to play more than 24, 25 minutes a game. In the aerial department William pays little attention to where the ball is. Russell owed a great deal of his rebounding to Heinsohn, who is forever blocking out, which automatically forces Russell's rebounding position."

Certainly the public perception of Russell in Boston wasn't helped by his persona—his size; his scowl; his refusal to sign autographs. Even his goatee, which he had started growing after his arrival, was a visible reminder that Russell was different in ways that went beyond his race and his size, goatees being associated then with jazz musicians and beatniks, people mainstream America viewed with a certain suspicion.

Would it have been different if he had been white?

No doubt.

Would it have been different if he'd had a different personality? Maybe. But that wasn't him. By the time of his arrival in Boston, he had already built a moat around himself and the outside world, a moat that few could ever cross. And he, of course, knew that both his size and his race intimidated people, two things he often used to his advantage, whether to keep fans away from him or to use as a competitive edge.

"I didn't ever care what people thought of me," he later said. "My mother taught me that some people will like you and some people will not like you. And that's on sight. And there's nothing you can do about it. So don't even try."

Nor was Russell's arrival into the NBA helped by his basketball home being Boston, a city whose racial problems would be laid out for all the world to see sixteen years later when the city would be the site for the worst school-busing crisis in American history.

Russell would be the first public figure to say that Boston was a racist city, that happening just a couple of years after his arrival. At the time that, too, had fallen on deaf ears, and by then he often was viewed as both difficult and angry, easy to dismiss.

And what was he talking about, anyway?

Hadn't Boston always been the cradle of American liberty, the "city on the hill," as John Winthrop, the first governor of the Massachusetts Bay Colony, had called it? Hadn't the city always been a cradle of liberty and culture, where the country's first public high school had opened as far back as 1635? Hadn't slavery been ruled unconstitutional way back in 1783? Hadn't Boston been the center of the abolition movement, with slavery outlawed as far back as the eighteenth century? Hadn't the schools been desegregated as far back as 1855? By the middle of the nineteenth century, had blacks not enjoyed a degree of freedom unprecedented in the country? Hadn't that been the goal way back in the nineteenth century, both the eradication of slavery in the South and the end of Northern discrimination?

What was Russell talking about?

That was the perception then, that Russell, all but impossible to deal with, was just an angry Negro throwing out accusations as though they were basketballs in a pregame shooting drill. A few years later, he would say that he and his family had difficulty buying a house in suburban Reading and that they had been the target of discrimination. Later, he would be viewed as a precursor to other athletes who politicized sports, one of the first to use his status as a platform, the voice crying out in the wilderness, a man who sometimes seemed back then to be on his own island. Later he would be seen as, if not exactly a visionary, certainly someone who never was going to politely embrace the status quo, arguably the most visible Negro athlete in the country to speak about race until the emergence of Cassius Clay.

"I have never worked to be well liked or well loved," he would write nine years later, "but only to be respected. I have fought a problem the only way I know how. Maybe it was right or wrong in the approach, but a man can only ultimately be counted if he thinks he is doing right. Then, at least, he is a man."

But by '57 there really were two Bostons. There was the idealized Boston, the one whose history was, in many ways, the history of the country, Lexington and Concord and Paul Revere's ride, the first public high school in the country, the first college in the country, the birthplace of the country's literary heritage, in many ways the birthplace of the country's culture. That was the Boston taught in the schoolbooks, the history the city held so dear. Then there was the other Boston, one of poor working-class neighborhoods separated by ethnicity, the Irish in South Boston, Charlestown, and Dorchester, the Italians in East Boston and the North End, the blacks in Roxbury. This was feudal Boston, one that might have existed in the shadows of the Brahmins on Beacon

Hill, but was light-years away in terms of lifestyle and attitudes, with its tough, ethnic politics, and its clannishness.

In the nineteenth century, many of Boston's blacks had been educated, closely aligned with whites. That had begun to change as the city's ethnic makeup changed. More blacks, uneducated and unskilled, arrived from the South, establishing distinct divisions in the black community. The poorer blacks competed for marginal jobs with the Irish, escalating tensions that would last for generations. From 1940 until 1957, the black population in Boston almost tripled as the influx of more uneducated Southern blacks flooded the city and settled into ghettos.

This was the Boston Russell encountered, and it was soon apparent he had little use for it, even if many in Boston saw that as heresy. Complicating everything was that by the time Russell arrived in Boston, the Red Sox had never had a black player and were owned by Tom Yawkey, owner of a plantation in South Carolina, whose lasting baseball reputation would be that he owned the last Major League team to integrate. That happened two and a half years after Russell first arrived in the city, when Elijah "Pumpsie" Green was called up from their Minneapolis farm team in June 1959. It was also fourteen years after the Red Sox had tried out Jackie Robinson and two other black ballplayers in Fenway Park. The tryout had been perfunctory at best, coming after a local politician had put pressure on the Red Sox, and ending when someone had yelled out from one of the boxes above, "Get those niggers off the field."

It was an incident that happened before Robinson had signed with the Brooklyn Dodgers; yet Robinson never forgot it, to the point that he later said Yawkey was one of the most bigoted men in baseball. The Red Sox also had sent a scout to watch Willie

Mays, then just a kid in Birmingham, Alabama, but the game got rained out, and rather than wait around to see Mays play, the scout left and later filed a report saying Mays couldn't play. It's also part of the Red Sox's unfortunate history that manager Pinky Higgins once in the fifties told a Boston sportswriter that there wouldn't be any black players on the team as long as he was the manager.

This was the sports climate Russell found himself in, one that was rarely questioned in the Boston of his time, and in many ways it was as much a reality to him in his first year as his adjustment to the NBA. There was little question that there wasn't a lot of nightlife for Negroes, save for a couple of nightclubs in Roxbury such as Slades and the Hi-Hat, leftovers from the time before World War II when the intersection of Massachusetts and Columbus avenues had been Boston's version of Harlem, filled with restaurants and clubs and nightlife. However, most of that was gone—just memories—by the time Russell came to Boston. Russell looked at Boston and saw few opportunities, feeling almost as if he were on an island. This was hardly surprising, considering that he was the only black professional athlete in a city with very few black professionals anywhere.

When Green arrived with the Red Sox in '59, he was quickly befriended by Russell, who sometimes would drive him around the city in his Lincoln Continental, all the while talking about how racist Boston was, how lonely and miserable he was, speaking in monologues as if he were sitting on some therapist's couch.

But since his arrival he had changed; of that there was no question. He was a preview of the future. He was not looking to be a "credit to his race," like the great prizefighter Joe Louis was acclaimed to be. Most of all, he was never going to play the fool, like some Negro out of an old minstrel show. He was educated, proud, and he knew what he believed. And nothing was going to get in the way of this, absolutely nothing.

"I had made up my mind that I would not become the bigot's stereotype of the Negro," he said in his first book, *Go Up for Glory*, which came out nine years later. "I would not be the laughing boy, seeking their favors. I would just be me. Take it any way you want to."

He also said in *Go Up for Glory* that he was less worried about how his teammates would accept him than how he would accept them. From the beginning he had liked Sharman, who had met him at the airport. The book emphatically makes the point that Auerbach was never close with any of the players, with the possible exception of Cousy, with whom he had made some summertime overseas trips, and that in the world of professional sports, it's the players who make the coach, not the other way around.

"In the locker room, Auerbach doesn't say much if you are winning," he writes. "He just advises to watch so and so and calls men in key plays or styles. If you are losing, occasionally he will start yelling: 'What is this goddamned thing? A prom or something? You all want to be dancers? The hell with it. Let's go home now. I don't want to watch you guys play basketball. You make me throw up.'"

Go Up for Glory is just one of several books Russell would later write, but it's the only one done when he was still playing, so it is more of an insider's book than the others, more raw, an autobiography by a man stating his personal manifesto, take it or leave it. The books that came later were more reflective, written by an older man trying to put his life in perspective, and while certainly powerful, the later books didn't have the same emotional wallop as *Go Up for Glory*.

"There are no alibis in this book," he says in the opening line. "It is a story that can be read on three levels. The story of an American. The story of a Negro. The story of a professional basketball player."

And there's this:

"You are a Negro. You are less."

He wrote about finding a book in the library when he was just a young kid and reading about a man named Henri Christophe, who once had led a slave uprising in Haiti. Russell explained how he had gained a certain pride from learning this.

"One night when I was 16 I went to bed just a boy," he writes. "I woke up the next morning proud—so very proud—to be a Negro. The pride has since been with me."

His relationship with the city of Boston would only get more complicated as the years went by. He would call the city racist and essentially want nothing to do with it. He was estranged from Boston for years, moving away in 1968 when his career ended, and having little to do with the city for decades, until coming back in a hugely symbolic moment in 1999 when he was honored in a ceremony in the FleetCenter, adjoining the old Garden. But he never had any trouble with his teammates, and from his arrival, in all the important ways, he was the perfect teammate. He played with an incredible determination and intensity. He was totally unselfish. He was always loyal to his teammates. He also grew to have a deep respect for Auerbach. Within the confines of the team, away from the sportswriters and the fans, he would laugh and joke and, to a certain extent, be one of the guys. His booming laugh was a loud cackle.

That was just one of the great contradictions of Russell, the sense that the side of him his teammates saw was so different than the one the public saw, even if Russell later said he hadn't been particularly close to anyone on the Celtics his first year, both because of his late arrival and the fact he had arrived guarded.

"Russ never responded to hecklers," Cousy said. "He would never even look at them. But inside the locker room he was laughing all the time. Russell always has been very outgoing when he feels comfortable. We didn't know how militant he was then."

Later, Russell would say that he never heard the hecklers because he never heard the cheers either, and that he played off in some private world that had nothing to do with what fans thought, one way or the other.

"He's friendly and easy with those he likes," Joe DeLauri, the Celtics' trainer in the late sixties, once told *Sports Illustrated* about those years when Russell was the player-coach. "But the big concern he has is for the Celtics. Nothing else matters. That's why he seems so cold often to the press and the fans. They're not Celtics. After we won the championship last year he kicked everyone who wasn't a Celtic out of the dressing room—press, photographers, hangers-on. . . . The press was pounding on the door, furious about deadlines and all, and Russell turned around and looked at us and he asked Bailey Howell to lead the team in prayer. He knew Bailey was a religious man—it was also his first year on a championship team—and he knew Bailey would appreciate it. Russell's not a religious man himself. Sam Jones said, 'You pray?' And Russell said, 'Yeah, Sam.'"

In time, Russell's greatness, his ability to control a game defensively, would become appreciated, but that took a lot of years and a lot of titles before he became universally recognized for his rare ability to influence a basketball game, the one constant on the Celtics as players came and went around him in the glory years of the fifties and sixties. It would take years before everyone would begin to see what Auerbach always had known, that for all the great talent that came through their locker room in those years, Russell was the reason the Celtics kept winning.

Even then, Russell's impact on a game took a certain appreciation, not only of his unique skills, but an understanding that the most valuable player didn't always have to be the high scorer, even though that was the way most people saw basketball.

Then again, his game always had been an acquired taste.

"He looked uncertain with himself offensively and in simple ballhandling," Cousy said.

He definitely didn't have any confidence in that part of his game. In his first few games, he routinely tried to take some jump shots, and he seemed to grow more uncertain, more tentative when they didn't go in, until Auerbach reminded him that he wasn't here to shoot jumpers, that he wasn't here to score, that his rebounds were being counted as baskets. But in one of his first games he'd been pushed around by the Knicks' Harry Gallatin, and he seemed tentative about fighting back. This was not surprising, considering he had missed training camp, plus almost the first two months of the season, and the NBA game was so much more physical than the college game had been. Plus, the Celtics had been rolling along when he joined them, in first place in the Eastern Division, and in the minds of the players he had to fit in with them, not the other way around.

Lapchick, the Knicks coach who was respected throughout the game, often said that every new player in the NBA was tested, one way or another, and it was how he responded to that test that determined everything.

So it was happening with Russell in his early games, primarily by stronger, older, more experienced players, who were going to try and beat up on him. He was miserable in the beginning, new to the city, new to the team, the only black, on the other side of the country from where he had grown up and gone to college, and he was in the beginnings of a marriage. He was almost late to his first game because he had gotten stuck in traffic inside the Sumner Tunnel.

And from the start he was a curiosity piece. Wherever the Celtics went, people came out to see him. On the road people heckled him, yelling insults and racial epithets. This also sometimes happened in the Boston Garden. On the court, opposing centers came after him.

This continued until there came a doubleheader in Syracuse, in a game against the Knicks, where he punched their center, the six-foot-eleven Ray Felix, knocking him out.

That was a watershed moment.

After that, other players started to back off.

He had been tested.

And he had passed the test.

Even if no one then knew how dominant he was to become, there was no question he was a curiosity piece. His debut in the Boston Garden had drawn eleven thousand people, the largest crowd of the season at the time, despite the game's having been televised. He almost tripled the attendance in his first visit to Fort Wayne and almost doubled it in Syracuse, despite a snowstorm.

In both Philadelphia and St. Louis, his appearance drew record crowds. He drew more than fifteen thousand people to Madison Square Garden in New York.

"From that cash-in-the till standpoint, then, Russell is worth his handsome salary," wrote Arthur Daley in the *New York Times* in February. "From an artistic standpoint he isn't entirely worth it—yet. But don't overlook that lonesome word, 'yet.'"

Daley was right. Soon the curiosity factor would dissipate. For too many fans he soon became just another big guy who couldn't shoot, valuable to his team certainly, but not someone you'd sit up in the third balcony to see, for the simple reason you had to understand basketball's nuances to fully appreciate Russell's greatness.

But it was there, no question about it. It was there in the sense that Russell immediately had made the Celtics the best team in basketball. It was the sense that he did things defensively that no one had even seen before, just as no one had ever seen a big man who could run and jump like he could. In this way alone, he was a glimpse at the game's future, how basketball would evolve, complete with bigger and more athletic men, many of them African-American. In this sense alone, Russell was a pioneer, the beginning of something impossible to understand in 1957.

Daley wrote how the size of the players in the league had been an adjustment for Russell—the fact that the average height in the league was six foot five. Russell said how he had no trouble establishing position in the low post in college, but in the pros it was more difficult, like pushing against a concrete wall.

"I could bluff 'em in college," he said with a wry smile. "I can't bluff 'em here."

He said how his reputation in college had helped him, but

not here. Here he was just a rookie, here to take the money out of some opponent's mouth, and the opponents pushed back. The article went on to quote Auerbach saying he knew right from the start Russell had been well coached in college, especially defensively, and had been accepted by his teammates. But about his shooting?

"Who the hell wants a guy six foot ten to shoot from beyond the foul line?" exploded Auerbach.

Daley's article also was one more example of the game's growth, for this was the staid *New York Times*, the old gray lady herself, the most prominent newspaper in the country, not only dealing with the NBA, but saying how the pro game was obviously a more competitive one than the college game, both bigger and full of ex-collegiate all-Americans.

"The pros have skinned the cream off the college crop," Daley wrote. "They have breathtaking shot-makers and play-makers. Some of the things they do strain credulity, such as Bob Cousy dribbling down court right-handed and then dribbling behind his back to break clear into a left-handed dribble."

It was one more reminder of the impact Russell already had made on the NBA, even if there was still speculation on what ultimately it would turn out to be.

"We drew great crowds and we were rolling and everywhere we went the gauntlet was cast down and the challenge was made," he said. "I was pushed. I pushed back. I was shoved. I shoved back. I started a little book on players, a mental thing. Who had to shoot right-handed? Who is only a shooter and a ball-hog and won't pass? Can I psyche them?"

Russell knew his ability to block shots was a tremendous psychological advantage, something not really recognized at the time.

No one really had blocked shots before, not in the way Russell was doing it. It wasn't even a stat that was recorded, never mind something that was appreciated. Hadn't players always been told not to leave their feet on defense? Hadn't that always been one of the game's cardinal sins? And here was this rookie who not only blocked shots, but used the threat of it as a weapon.

So he would block an opponent's shot, and that would change things, that player forever aware of where Russell was on the floor. Was he close enough to get another one? Where was he this time? Russell knew he couldn't block all the shots. He also knew he didn't have to. Just the idea that he might had changed the equation.

"Actually, it's difficult to measure Bill's defensive value," said Phil Woolpert, his college coach, "because much of it is psychological—a shooter hurrying a shot he shouldn't take in order to avoid him, or not taking one he should take."

His teammates began referring to Russell's blocked shots as "Wilsonburgers," as the basketballs they played with were Wilsons. They knew they were seeing something unique, that Russell was doing something never done before; he knew he was changing the Celtics, the missing piece they had always needed.

"Russ allowed my playmaking abilities to express themselves fully," Cousy said. "All of a sudden I didn't have to be quite as careful. It wasn't like every damn pass was life and death out there. Now we could afford to gamble, whether it was in passing, shooting, or playing defense, and when you can play that way, when you're doing your thing, you're going to be better. That's what Russell gave us."

So became the Celtics of legend, the Celtics as arguably the first modern NBA team. Russell would get the rebound, throw the outlet to Cousy, and off the Celtics would go. It was as if Cousy were the conductor of the best orchestra in the world, pointing to the string section here, the horns there, knowing that wherever he decided to go with the ball, it was going to be sweet, sweet music. Cousy might have been better known for his freewheeling style, all the around-the-back stuff that was being imitated in every school yard in America, but here on the break was Cousy at his best, the place where he was a true basketball magician, with Sharman on one side, and Heinsohn on the other, and maybe Ramsey coming up behind him. This was the Celtics changing the game from the slow-plodding game in all those old gyms in the Midwest to the high-flying game it would become. This was the modern-day point guard knowing where all his teammates were on the court, knowing not to give the ball to Loscutoff in the open court where he had to take too many dribbles and not to give Russell the ball when he had to take any dribbles, and knowing how to go through all these permutations in the wink of an eye.

That was the other thing about the '57 Celtics; whether by accident, by Auerbach's vision, or a mixture of both, the players complemented one another. This was a preview of basketball's future.

Would it have been different if Russell had come in wanting to score, wanting to show the world what all the fuss had been about in college?

No doubt.

The secret of the Celtics was that their two highest profile players, Cousy and Russell, were defined as basketball players by something other than scoring. Cousy was defined by his passing and ballhandling wizardry; Russell by his rebounding and shot-blocking. This would have been unique for a high school team, let alone for the best team in basketball. Here was the best basketball team in the world, and its two best players were unselfish.

In a certain sense they all were, or if not exactly unselfish, well aware that their individual success depended on the others. Maybe that was because Cousy and Sharman had been great for years, but they had come to know they needed the rebounding that Russell gave them and the scoring help that both Heinsohn and Ramsey gave them to finally become a great team. Maybe it was because Russell knew he wasn't a great scorer, the first basketball superstar who wasn't. He was particularly embarrassed by his shooting woes that first season, being only a 49 percent foul shooter. Maybe it was because Heinsohn knew that for him to be at his best, he needed Cousy to get him the ball. It was as if they all intuitively came to know that to be a truly great team they all needed one another.

Maybe it was as simple as this, a theory Russell later talked about in his 1979 memoir, *Second Wind*.

"I wanted to lead the league in rebounding," he said. "Cousy wanted to lead the league in assists. Sharman wanted to lead the league in free throw percentage. Heinsohn wanted to lead the league in field goals taken. Auerbach wanted to lead the league in technical fouls and fines. The good thing about it was that no two Celtics had the same goals, and that nobody was trying to play the wrong role."

Virtually as soon as he arrived in Boston and joined the Celtics, he understood they were all about winning, not individual achievement, something he immediately embraced. In his sophomore year at San Francisco, the team had been riddled with dissension, so he had learned early what a cancer that was. He also had learned in college something he called "team ego," something that had evolved out of his frustration with not being recognized as much as he thought he should have been. The most symbolic slight had happened his senior year when even though he clearly had been the most dominant college player in the country, a player from nearby Santa Clara named Kenny Sears had been picked the player of the year in his conference over him. It hadn't been the only slight. The year before, he had come in second to La Salle's Tom Gola as the national player of the year. He viewed both these slights as racist. But they also taught him a valuable lesson: Winning was not subjective.

"Well, that let me know that if I were to accept these as the final judges of my career, I would die a bitter old man," he would say years later. "So I made a conscious decision: What I'll do is I will try my very best to win every game."

If his team won, no one could ever question his contribution. If his team won, no one could ever minimize his impact. It wouldn't be a coach's opinion. It wouldn't be a sportswriter's opinion. It wouldn't be anyone's opinion. It would be a historical fact: Bill Russell's teams won these games. So his ego as a basketball player, which he always admitted was a large one, became not an individual ego, but a team one. He would not only be viewed by how his team did, but that was the way he would also define himself.

"Do you know the difference between your ego and mine?" he told the Celtics team in 2001, a conversation he wrote about in *Russell Rules*. "My ego is not a personal ego. It's a team ego. My ego demands the success of my team. My personal achievements became my team's achievements."

Another occurrence in his early days with the Celtics that immediately told him what kind of a culture he was joining happened after a practice.

When Russell had joined the Celtics, the starting center had been Arnie Risen, who was nicknamed "Stilts." If Russell was the NBA's future, Risen was its past. He was six foot nine but was only 210 pounds, in many ways a typical big man in the basketball of the forties and fifties. It was an era in which the men were tall before their time, previews of what basketball would become, even though, so much taller than the people around them, they were often seen as almost misfits. Risen had played at Ohio State and had led the Buckeyes to Final Four appearances in '44 and '45, before signing a contract with the Indianapolis Kautskys of the National Basketball League, a pro league mainly in the Midwest. Two years later he was in the NBA with the Rochester Royals. There he was a four-time All-Star in the first half of the fifties, a main reason for the Royals' winning NBA titles in both '51 and '52.

Risen was a dominant player in his era, eventually being named to the Basketball Hall of Fame, and Auerbach had brought him in in '55 at the tail end of his career. It was something Auerbach would do throughout his career, acquiring veterans at the end of their careers, players who knew both the NBA game and what it took to be effective in it. He had done it before with both Risen and guard Andy Phillip, who came in to spell both Cousy and Sharman in the backcourt in '57. He had faith in them in ways he never had with rookies, and he was able to convince them to come to Boston, play on a good team, and prolong their careers for a year or two. They, in turn, knew what they had signed up for. Complaining about a lack of playing time wasn't it.

But maybe Risen's lasting contribution to the Celtics happened after Russell's first practice. Risen knew that Russell's arrival had changed his world with the Celtics, that Russell was going to play, and he was going to sit and watch. He could have resented it. He could have simply said nothing. He could have left all the coaching up to Auerbach. Instead, he took this young Negro rookie, this man who was going to send him to the bench forever, and told him about the opposing centers he was going to go up against, and tips on how to play them.

It was something Russell never forgot. It also reinforced for him that the Celtics were all about winning.

The Hawks were a confident team.

They already had beaten the Celtics in the Boston Garden, and there was little question they were a better team now than they were in the middle of the season. One reason was the emergence of Hagan, which two things had contributed to in one of those little twists of fate.

He had begun the year as a guard, since he was only six foot four, and Holzman had considered him too small to be an NBA forward, even though he always had been a forward in his great college career at Kentucky. But he didn't handle the ball well, and his basketball destiny seemed for him to be just another college star whose game didn't translate into the pros, the classic "tweener."

Then Hannum became the coach and made him a forward.

Pettit then broke his wrist, which gave Hagan playing time.

He immediately took advantage of it, to the point that he was now averaging 14 points a game in the play-offs when his season average had been only 6. He was strong and explosive, jumped well, and could even throw a running hook shot in the lane. It all made him difficult to guard, and when he came off the bench, it gave the Hawks a different look, just as did Ramsey's entrance into the Celtics' lineup. Now whenever Hagan was set to come in, Auerbach put Ramsey in to match up with him, so these two former Kentucky teammates were now going against each other in the NBA Finals.

"He's a great basketball player," Ramsey said. "Kind of fellow you have to be patient with. I know he acts like he's listless on the court. Anything but that is true. I know a lot about that boy, liked him, and spent a lot of time with him when we were at Kentucky for four years. I expect I know every move he makes out there."

"Remember, he spent two years in service and is just working out of it," said Hannum. "I rate Hagan one of the best prospects. And he's strong. He'll jump with the big men and if there's any battle for the ball, and Hagan is in the battle, he'll get that ball for us. We knew about these other players on the Hawks, but being a rookie, Hagan had to show us. He did."

And the Hawks had Pettit.

"In his day, Pettit was the best power forward there was," Auerbach would later say, adding that Pettit's ability to also play some center, and his relentlessness as a rebounder, made him the best. "Pettit was Mr. Clean, Mr. All America. He was a clean liver and a super guy, but very, very competitive. He would play all out 50 points ahead or behind. It didn't matter, that's the only way he knew how to play."

If Cousy and Russell both had become unlikely superstars, given their high school careers, so was Pettit, this man who'd been cut from his high school team, only staying with the game because his father, the sheriff of East Baton Rouge Parish, encouraged him to practice on the hoop in their backyard. So he spent hour after hour doing that, and by his senior year he led Baton Rouge High School to its first state title in more than two decades, and he was offered a scholarship at nearby Louisiana State University.

It was there that Pettit began a storybook career that would twice see him become an all-American, leading the Southeast Conference in scoring for three straight seasons. He had grown to six foot nine by then, averaged an incredible 31 points a game his senior year, and had been the first pick of the Milwaukee Hawks in 1954.

Still, there were some doubts whether this was going to translate into the NBA. He had been a center at LSU where he had essentially played with his back to the basket, and there were some questions about his strength at the professional level. These questions were soon answered as he became the rookie of the year, averaging 20 points a game, the fourth best in the league that season, and became the first rookie in the NBA's short history to make the all-league team.

More surprisingly, he had done that by transforming himself into a forward, someone who could score facing the basket.

"He was the most graceful big man I've ever seen," said Willie Naulls, his teammate for a brief while before being traded to the New York Knickerbockers.

In the April issue of New York–based *Sport* magazine, writer Al Silverman had profiled him in a story titled "Bob Pettit: The Big Man of Basketball." The story began with a scene of Pettit filming a television commercial for a cigarette on the top floor of a New York City armory, even though Pettit didn't smoke. Pettit was described as a "good-looking youngster with a boyish, handsome face, and a fine, well-proportioned big man's face," someone who reacted to success "with a modesty that can only be classified as refreshing."

It said that he had done some commercials for Ford the year before, and that Pettit now had the same agent who also represented Cousy. So it was obvious that Pettit, now only in his third year of pro ball, was already on the highest rung of the game.

"Cousy, who is the highest paid player in the game, gets an annual check in excess of $22,000," the article said. "Pettit, who was the second-highest-salaried player in the league before the Celtics acquired Bill Russell, gets an estimated $18,000."

Holzman, who had started the season as the Hawks' coach, said the key to Pettit's greatness was that he kept developing his game, going from someone who shot a lot of hook shots in college to someone who now had a great jump shot, his game getting more versatile every season.

"He'll probably be one of the all-time greats in the league," Holzman said. "The kid's got quite a few things that others don't have, like pride. He has a great deal of pride in himself. He's a perfectionist. It's the old story. He's the last guy out of the gym. I say to him, 'What are you doing, Bob?' And he'll say, 'I need some shots.' Yeah, he's the one guy who doesn't. He's a hell of a thinker. Got an awful lot of pride in what he does."

Holzman went on to say that when the Hawks had drafted him, they never expected him to be as good as he'd turned out to be. "We didn't hope that anybody could be that good," a sentiment Pettit shared.

"I was a little uncertain about making pro at all," he said. "It's something you really don't know. Most any player believes in himself to a certain degree. But you have to play it, try it. I was very,

very lucky. In college I played the standing pivot. My back was to the basket. In the pros, I'm always outside. Everything I do is facing the basket now. That was my chief difficulty in adjusting, the fact I had never played forward before."

Then there was the schedule.

The NBA played a seventy-two game schedule, three times the game colleges played, not counting exhibitions and play-offs that could push it up to one hundred. Pettit already had found, in this, only his third season, that it was not a particularly glamorous life; it was also difficult to find any kind of routine. In St. Louis, he and teammate Med Park, a reserve guard who had played at the University of Missouri, shared what was referred to as a "bachelor apartment," even doing their own cooking; yet the article said that in the off-season he still lived with his parents. It also said that two years earlier he already had started his own insurance agency in Baton Rouge, and that he already was thinking about his future after the game, that although he liked St. Louis, he missed his life back in Louisiana.

"I still love the game, still love to play," Pettit said. "I've never gotten to the point where I didn't love it, even if the traveling is kind of rough. It's a tremendous challenge every night. You're playing against the greatest players in the world. But I wouldn't want to drag it out. This is my third year. I may not play anymore after this year, or I may play two or three years. The way I feel now, though, I don't want to play for any 10 years."

The Hawks' backcourt comprised Slater Martin and Jack McMahon, two tough defensive players who, though certainly overmatched in offensive talent by Cousy and Sharman, always made things difficult for them.

McMahon had starred at St. John's, where he had been the

captain of a team that went 24–5 and made it to the NCAA Tournament. He had broken into the NBA with the Rochester Royals, where he had been a teammate of Risen's, and had come to the Hawks two years earlier. There was nothing flashy about his game, and he wasn't much of a scorer, but he was as tough as his native New York, one of those guys often referred to as a "pro's pro." Eventually, he became a coach and ultimately was in the NBA for thirty-seven years, but in this series his job was to shadow Sharman and get the ball to Pettit, Macauley, and Hagan. Blattner called him "Irish" on his radio broadcasts.

"We'll see you in the play-offs," he had told the Celtics in their last visit to Boston in late February.

Martin was the very definition of feisty, the ultimate overachiever, someone who had led his high school team to back-to-back Texas state titles in the forties, before going off to star at the University of Texas where he once scored 49 points in a game. Nicknamed "Dugie," in the NBA he was one of those disciplined, steady playmakers who didn't shoot much, but knew how to run a team, a pro's pro. He had done that on the championship Lakers teams before ending up with the Hawks in 1956, after Kerner shrewdly had worked out a deal to get him from the Lakers, by way of a few days with the Knicks. He was only about five foot ten, but he was quick and, along with Al Cervi of the Syracuse Nationals, played Cousy as well as anyone did and took great pride in that.

He had once heard a Minneapolis front office person say the Lakers had been so good up front during the Mikan years, they could win with two bellhops in the backcourt; yet he was appreciated on the Hawks. Before his arrival, they had been bothered by pressing defenses and by their inability to get the ball into their frontcourt players, especially Pettit.

"When we get pressed, just give me the ball and get out of the way," Martin had said when he arrived, and his presence immediately made the Hawks better.

Yet he also had tremendous respect for both Cousy and Sharman.

"I think the same way a lot of people feel," he said. "Cousy and Sharman are the finest backcourt I've ever seen. Cousy is a great ballplayer. I feel that if he is stopped, the Celtics are stopped. He's their ball club as far as I'm concerned. I worry about nobody else on that court when I'm on it with Cousy."

Still, Martin was never going to give an inch.

He claimed he had never had his ankles taped in his life, but just "put on my jockstrap" and went out to play.

"Hell, we didn't even have a trainer," he once said, long after his career was over. "If you got hurt bad, they had to ask for a doctor to come out of the stands. Is there a doctor in the house? I saw players play with bones hanging out."

Once, before a game against the Celtics, he told Cousy, "Any of those fancy behind-your-backs tonight, Cousy, and I'll kick your ass at midcourt in front of all these fans."

Cousy was not a jump shooter, not someone who was going to create his own shot in a half-court offense. Nor was he considered a great shooter, not in any pure sense of the word. He was, though, viewed as someone who would make big shots, the money shots that decided games. There was the theory that although he could be having a bad shooting night, he would still make the big shot that broke an opponent's heart. He had a one-hander that he could shoot from deep, a shot he could utilize successfully if he could get his defender to go behind the screen, but he hadn't been shooting it particularly well going into this series, the result of ending the season with a bit of a banged-up knee. Against most defenders he could use his superior quickness to get to the screen a step ahead, forcing them to go underneath the screen. That was difficult to do with Martin, who was just as quick as Cousy, and who always seemed to get over the screen on Cousy.

Yet Cousy had had big scoring games in the first six games of the series, as had Sharman and Heinsohn. This was the Celtics' strength, the scoring ability of Heinsohn and Ramsey up front, and Cousy and Sharman in the backcourt, much of it the result of their ability to get out and run and get easy shots. In turn, the Hawks relied on their big frontcourt to score, specifically Pettit, Hagan, and Macauley.

It was front-page news in the *Boston Globe* on April 13, 1957, that the Red Sox were going to open their Fenway Park season in an exhibition game against the Phillies. Manager Mike "Pinky" Higgins, who later would be remembered in Boston sports history as a virulent racist, said that he was bringing a "tighter infield" into a new season, and that Ted Williams was scheduled to play. But the game already had been cancelled due to forecasted cold weather, and the word was that several of the Red Sox players were going to go to the Celtics game.

The Celtics also were on the front page.

CAPACITY CROWD TO SEE NBA PLAYOFF GAME, screamed the headline across the top of a page in the *Boston Globe* sports section in big black type. CELTS EYE HAPPY ENDING TO 11-YEAR QUEST, the sub-head said.

The article, written by Jack Barry, said that in the recent "money games," the Hawks had won the close ones. Barry called Heinsohn the most consistent performer of the first six games, even if Hagan had eluded him for the winning tip-in in the sixth game. Barry then commented, "This is just what Heinsohn has been doing to old pros like Ed Macauley and Earl Lloyd and others during the last nine games."

Barry also wrote that the Celtics should stop bickering about the referees since it wasn't the refs who had turned the ball over twenty-eight times in the sixth game, the underlying theme being that if they lost, the Celtics would have no one to blame but themselves.

This was a theme pounded the day before in the *Globe* by Clif Keane, his theory being that they should get over their growing obsession with the referees, specifically Sid Borgia, who the Celtics believed didn't like them, and always would go out of his way to stick it to them on a big call in a key moment. Then again, Keane and Auerbach were forever circling around each other like alley cats, the legacy of Auerbach's slighting Cousy back in 1950 and Keane's never having let him forget it.

"The clock didn't beat the Celtics last night," Keane wrote. "Referee Sid Borgia didn't, either. They just plain whipped themselves—and unless they get over their grouch against Sid Borgia, they stand to be whipped at the Garden tomorrow afternoon."

The Celtics were upset that they already had seen Borgia in five out of the six games, even though they had put him last on their list for the nine officials scheduled to work the series. He seemingly had been around forever, having begun refereeing in the NBA's first year. Behind his back he was called "the king of the makeup call," but there was no question he had a big personality. He called many players by their first names, and later would say that there was never any real NBA rule book and that NBA referees used the college rules as a base and then improvised. Since there were no game tapes, and few games on television, the referees could do what they wanted, the trick being to keep fouls even, so at the end of the game no one had a bitch. That was the theory, anyway. Even so, Auerbach and Borgia always seemed to be in the middle of some feud, dating back to the late forties. In many ways they were mirror images of each other, both five foot nine, combative, and stars in their own movie.

"I was a very emotional referee," Borgia would say years later, "and I was a very proud referee. If anything happened during the course of a game, which I felt was belittling to me or my profession, I became very belligerent. And if it happened in Boston, of course, the crowd was all over me, and that, in my mind, was a form of intimidation, so I became stronger and stronger. Goddamn it, no one was going to intimidate Sid Borgia on the job. Nobody.

"So now we come to the Redhead. Red would do every trick in the book to upset the officials, to harass them, to intimidate them. Now frankly, I wouldn't give you a nickel for any coach who wouldn't bitch when he thought he had a bitch coming. But every time I blew my whistle, he thought he had one coming. And he'd elaborate on it immediately.

"Whenever I'd try and explain my point of view to him, it always ended up with him telling me, 'You're full of shit.' It never failed. And because he was so damned loud, everybody in the joint heard it, so that's when I'd call the technical. It was embarrassing to me. Not only that, but if he got away with it, everybody in the league would be telling me I'm full of shit."

Auerbach was constantly telling his players not to challenge Borgia, to let him think he was in charge. They also were upset that referee Mendy Rudolph, whom the Hawks didn't like, had only worked three times in the six games.

Rudolph, who later would be regarded as one of the best refs in NBA history, had entered the league in 1953 after having started doing games in the Eastern League when he was just twenty years old. Years later he would admit to a compulsive gambling problem. Although he would admit he'd been offered money to erase some of his debts by point-shaving, he stressed he had never done that; he loved the game too much. He was Jewish, but having a swarthy complexion with jet-black hair, he was mercilessly taunted in St. Louis by fans who undoubtedly assumed he was "nonwhite." Whatever the reason, the Hawks always thought Rudolph was out to get them, all but cringing at the sight of him.

No matter.

The two refs for the game were Borgia and Rudolph, one the Celtics perceived to be always against them, and one the Hawks thought was always against them.

Regardless of the referees, the subtext on this Saturday in April was that the Celtics were undergoing a crisis of confidence. This was partly the result of the supposed internal bickering that had gone on after Hagan's tip-in against Heinsohn that had won the sixth game for the Hawks. It was also the result of Brown's statement that if the Celtics didn't win, some heads were going to roll and Auerbach's wouldn't be among them. The bickering and Brown's statement were manifestations of the pressure, of course. The Celtics were so close—just a game away—to what they had been chasing for so long; yet every time they seemed ready to reach out and grab this title that everyone a couple of weeks ago thought was going to be theirs, something seemed to happen. It was as if the basketball gods were yet to be convinced.

Heinsohn would later say he didn't realize then, in his first year, what winning the NBA title meant to Cousy and Sharman, because he simply had been too young. But in a certain sense winning was even more important to Auerbach and Brown, the two who knew how precarious the franchise's financial situation always had been and who also knew the realities of the pro game in ways the players did not.

It really had been a long quest for those who had been around in all those times when the Garden had been two-thirds full at best. It had been a long quest for those who had spent so many years overshadowed by both the Red Sox and the Bruins, all the while knowing they had a great game, if only more people in Boston would realize it. Finally they were getting their chance, but now this series, which many people had viewed as little more than a coronation for the Celtics, was down to one game. It was one game that not only meant so much for the Celtics, but it would also come to mean so much more in ways greater and more far-reaching than then imaginable.

There also was a story in the *Boston Globe* that morning that spoke of the economic realities of the league, even in the midst of what were being called the greatest Finals in NBA history. Written by Keane, it said that the gross receipts of the series would be in the vicinity of $150,000, far and away a new play-off high in NBA history. With the winning team expecting to get $18,000 and the losing team $15,000, roughly $117,000 remained.

Where was that going to go?

Some was going to Commissioner Podoloff and the league office in New York City. The rest was going to owners Brown and Kerner, much to the consternation of the players.

"We will get about $800 apiece after all the shares are distributed," several of the Celtics told Keane, though none were named by Keane in the newspaper article. "That would mean about $200 a week during the play-offs, less than we receive in the season. There is a lot of prestige to it. But prestige doesn't help pay any rent anywhere."

Kerner replied, "It's true the play-offs have made money," he said, "but remember that there are still some teams in this league losing money, or [they] did until they moved and we'll have to see what happens to them in the future. I have been in basketball for eleven years. I have paid out about a million in salaries over those years. I haven't made money—far from it. Who was worrying about me in those days?

"Certainly, there will be changes made if this continues to improve as it has this year. But right now we were only able to give what we thought we could pay."

Money was on everyone's mind, though.

There was speculation that, given their success, both Heinsohn and Russell would be asking for raises in the off-season—and maybe Cousy and Sharman, too, as once again they both had been named to the all-NBA first team. It was estimated in the *Boston Evening American* that Sharman was making $15,000 and Cousy $22,000. The gist of the story was that the Celtics had had their best year ever at the gate, with twenty-five regular home games, three in Providence, Rhode Island, and six home play-off games, but that Brown had said at a recent basketball luncheon that he still must get added revenue to "keep the Celtics above water financially."

He had even floated the idea of turning the Garden court around, a move that would add more seats on the floor. He had indicated he might try anything to get more revenue, especially in a year in which he figured several of his players were going to come looking for more money, even though he already had the largest payroll in the league.

But hovering over everything on this morning was the feeling that the Celtics had squandered their big opportunity to close out the series in the sixth game in St. Louis, complete with the reality that in the three close games, the so-called money games, the Hawks had won all of them.

This was the baggage the Celtics brought to the seventh game, a game that was both about their history, and about this particular team. Although so talented, the team was finding it so very difficult to put away the Hawks and so difficult to get its first championship. It almost seemed it was the Celtics' fate for its members to always be close, but never the ultimate winners, their fate to get upset by the St. Louis Hawks in this year that was supposed to have been theirs.

"Within a few hours after play-off tickets for today' game went on sale at the Garden yesterday, all but the poorest seats were sold, proving once again that the Celtics have a large and loyal following," wrote Larry Claflin in the *Boston Evening American*. "But one wonders how long the fans of Boston will support a team that always pulls out the crying towel when it loses." The title on his column this afternoon was "Celts by 8 points," that being the betting line.

He also said the Hawks were going to start Pettit, Hagan, Coleman, Martin, and McMahon, the same five who had started the sixth game in St. Louis, and that their strategy was to stay in the game and try to steal it in the end, the same formula that had given them their three wins.

"There was so much complaining from the Celtics players and their coach this week that they are getting the reputation of the biggest bunch of babies since the 1940 Cleveland Indians," Claflin wrote. "Perhaps they are right in their constant charge that the referees in the NBA, particularly Sid Borgia, are against them but it is a charge that cannot be proved and the more they complain the less attention anyone will pay them."

Claflin also pointed out that the constant bickering about referees, as well as Auerbach's fist fight with Kerner, had taken some of the luster off the best played and richest final in NBA history.

He also lashed out at Podoloff, "the president of this sometimes dizzy league," who had a sharp tongue and seemed to lack the dignity to be a president of a major sports league. Claflin observed that before the fifth game in the Garden, Podoloff had stood in the lobby and argued with fans about officials.

"With teams moving into Cincinnati and Detroit next season, the NBA is truly big-time now," he wrote. "The conduct of some of the coaches, a few of the players, and even one or two of the owners is not big league."

But this game was going to be, one way or the other.

For that was one of the other things buried at the end of Jack Barry's story in the *Boston Globe*, the news that the Celtics hoped to have their annual "break-up party" at the Garden club the following night at seven o'clock, win or lose.

Win or lose.

CHAPTER TWELVE

In the end there would be an incredible thirty-two lead changes, and the game would be tied twenty-eight times. In the end the game would always be called one of the greatest final games in NBA history.

But no one knew that at two thirty on a Saturday afternoon when the game began in a sold-out Boston Garden, with 13,909 spectators. It all seemed a long way from the "Milkman's Special" of just five years ago, a game that had started after midnight, one of Brown's promotions. It seemed so far from the days when the Eastern Massachusetts high school tournament outdrew the Celtics in the Garden.

There were three players on the NBA first team in the game, Cousy, Sharman, and Pettit, the other two that year being Paul Arizin of the Philadelphia Warriors and Syracuse's Schayes. Arizin, Pettit, and Schayes were the three top scorers in the league, and Sharman and Cousy were seventh and eighth. Russell was fourth in the league in rebounding, a category Rochester's Maurice Stokes won, although Russell's average of 19.6 a game was the highest.

From the beginning the game lived up to its hype.

Or as described in the *New York Times* the next day, "The game produced splendid basketball by both teams. The action was so feverish that the fans were left limp when that last buzzer sounded."

Each team brought incredible energy and intensity, and in many ways the seventh game resembled the first game, the one the Hawks had won in double overtime. There was no doubt the Hawks believed they could win, Boston Garden or no Boston Garden. They also knew that all the pressure was on the Celtics. In many ways the Hawks had a free pass, a game they were not supposed to win, but already had proved they could.

The Hawks led after the first quarter, 28–26, nullifying the quick start the Celtics had gotten off to.

By halftime the Hawks still led by two, 53–51, the pressure intensifying on the Celtics.

The Celtics were up 83–77 at the end of the third quarter, seemingly about to take control.

Then the real game started.

It was almost as if the first three quarters had merely been foreplay, the sparring of two quality prizefighters before the real fight started, lending credence to the old adage about the NBA that you really only had to watch the last two minutes. Every time it looked as if the Celtics were finally going to take control, the Hawks would somehow find a way to come clawing back, a microcosm of the series, a game played with a certain fury.

As the game got down to the closing minutes, the Hawks were up four and appeared to have the game in control, only to have the

Celtics, with the help of the roaring crowd, come back with three free throws to only trail by one, 101–100. The Garden crowd was in a frenzy, the cheers thundering down from the upper balconies. It had all come down to this—the trade for Russell, the long season, all the years of trying to convince the city of Boston that the Celtics were worth caring about and cheering for; all those years of Brown counting the house and wondering whether the Celtics were ever going to make it at the box office; all those years Cousy and Sharman had been great, only to eventually lose in the playoffs because the team simply wasn't big enough; all those nights of Auerbach in his hotel room with his Chinese food and wondering if he was ever going to win the big one.

It had all come down to this: They were down one.

The game was now inside a minute. Then the Hawks' Jack Coleman, a six-foot-seven forward in his ninth year in the NBA out of Louisville, received an outlet pass at midcourt and seemed to be on his way to an open layup that would have given the Hawks a commanding 3-point lead. He was clearly ahead of everyone on the floor. Coleman was from Kentucky and owned his own farm, called "The Old Rancher" by many of the people around the Hawks.

And here he was about to make the defining play of the NBA Finals.

Not Pettit, the Hawks' superstar.

Not Hagan, their emerging rookie scorer.

Not Macauley, the ex-Celtic.

Not their experienced backcourt.

But Jack Coleman.

Then came Russell.

Out of nowhere.

Starting underneath the far basket when he saw Coleman get the ball at midcourt, he set out to catch Coleman with his huge strides. He flew by Heinsohn, who had been standing near midcourt, then caught him at the rim and blocked his shot.

"It was the most incredible physical act I ever saw on a basketball floor," Cousy would say years later. "I had just led him down the floor and he had missed a shot, but his momentum had carried him off the court. Then I looked up and Coleman already had an outlet pass at midcourt and he had four or five steps on everybody. He was going to score and they were going to go up three with about forty seconds left to play. Russell took off with those loping steps and they must have been six or seven of the longest steps ever seen. He covered the entire 94 feet in no time at all and blocked Coleman's shot. Coleman was no speed demon, but he was very athletic and could move."

"I saw nobody was going after him, so I went after him," Russell would later say. "So I caught him and blocked his shot and kept it in play."

"Blocked by Russell! Blocked by Russell! He came from nowhere," Johnny Most yelled over the radio. "Blocked by Russell."

"It was the most athletic play I ever saw in basketball," Heinsohn would say decades later.

Coleman would say there was no way Russell could have blocked the shot without goaltending.

No matter.

The Celtics were still alive, courtesy of a play that seemed to come out of basketball's future, as if someone had put a tape of a contemporary NBA game into the VCR. This was the kind of play no one in basketball had ever seen before—a six-foot-ten man running the length of the court as if he were a sprinter, then having the jumping ability to block Coleman's shot without crashing into him and fouling him.

If anyone still had doubt they were looking at something different when they watched Russell play, this had to erase it. No one else on the court on that April afternoon in the Boston Garden could have made that play.

What would basketball one day evolve into?

The answer was all there in that one incredible defensive play by Russell, if anyone was prescient enough to connect the dots. The answer was there, just as it had been ever since Russell's arrival in December, his arrival being the reason why the Celtics were in the NBA Finals to begin with.

And with just thirteen seconds left, the Celtics up one, Cousy was at the foul line for two shots. If he made them both, the Celtics would win, as if it were all preordained, a script written by the basketball gods. Bob Cousy, who had been there since 1950 and had carried the Celtics for so many years both at the gate and on the court, the guy Auerbach initially hadn't wanted, the longtime darling of the Garden's galleries, was going to make the two game-winning free throws and bring the first NBA title to the Boston Celtics. Could there have been a better ending?

He made the first.

The Celtics were now up two with just thirteen seconds left in a league that was two decades away from the three-point shot. If he made the second free throw, it would seem virtually impossible for the Hawks to tie the game, needing an improbable three-point play in the dying seconds.

The Hawks called a time-out.

Suddenly, Cousy was nervous. He hadn't really been nervous in a basketball game since his junior year back at Andrew Jackson

High School in Queens, when being in a real game still had been new to him. Hadn't that always been one of his strengths, his ability to block everything else out, the crowd, his emotions, the pressure, all of it? Hadn't he played so many big games in his career, both in college and the NBA, when so many times he had come through in the clutch? Hadn't he always been able to go to some private place, someplace for just him and the ball, someplace where he could exert control?

He had not had a good shooting game, finishing only 5 for 20 from the field. None of that mattered now. All he had to do was make a free throw, something he had been doing throughout his career. With just him and the ball and the basket only fifteen feet away, the Celtics were all but guaranteed to win.

The Celtics were in a huddle during the time-out, Auerbach giving instructions on what to do after Cooz made the foul shot, because everyone knew Cooz was going to make the foul shot. That was a given, even though all he could think about was what was going to happen if he missed.

And he did, of course.

He missed so badly that his shot didn't even hit the rim, what he would call a "pure and complete choke."

The Hawks got the ball back, and in the dying seconds, Pettit drove on Russell and was fouled.

Pettit stepped to the foul line in the cacophonous din that was the Boston Garden and made the two free throws as if he were still a kid shooting baskets in his backyard in Baton Rouge, back when his head was full of basketball dreams and far-off fantasies of one day making big foul shots in big games in big arenas. He made the two free throws. The game was headed to overtime tied at 103 apiece.

The Hawks quickly went up four in the second overtime, but the Celtics tied it again on two Ramsey baskets. After a Sharman score gave them a lead, Coleman eluded Russell this time. His basket with just ten seconds to play left the game heading into a second overtime, tied at 113.

After Russell scored on a layup and Heinsohn made another long jumper, Heinsohn fouled out.

He had scored 37 points and garnered 23 rebounds. He had a game that would live forever in Celtics' history. But none of those things were on his mind. He left the game in tears. He first headed for the runway behind the scorer's table that led to the Celtics' locker room, because he wasn't sure of what to do, or even where to go, only to turn around and go back to the bench. He wrapped a towel around his head, then buried his head between his knees, completely spent. He stayed there for the rest of the game, never looking up, lost in his own thoughts, even when there was a time-out and all the other players surrounded Auerbach on the court. All the while Heinsohn continued to sit on the bench, a lonely sentinel in a war that wasn't over yet.

Ramsey canned a twenty-footer with just a minute and fifteen seconds left that put the Celtics up three.

Again the Hawks fought back.

Martin made a foul shot, then reserve guard Med Park made another, and with just twenty-three seconds left, the Hawks were only down one and they had the ball.

In the game was Hannum, who still always wore a uniform even after he became the coach, occasionally putting himself in games. He had been in the game for the past two and half minutes, ever since Macauley fouled out, for it had come down to him and a little-known reserve named Irv Bemoras. Bemoras, however, was only six foot three, so Hannum had chosen himself. He was thrown a bullet pass, and in trying to control it, was called for traveling by Rudolph, the referee the Hawks disliked the most in the league.

The ball went over to the Celtics, and Hannum fouled Loscutoff, in the game for the departed Heinsohn.

But just one second remained.

The Celtics up one.

Loscutoff, sandy-haired and tough, was six foot five and weighed 220. Two years earlier he had replaced Brannum as the Celtics' enforcer, one of the guys whose job was both to protect Cousy and Sharman and give the Celtics a degree of toughness. He was the Celtics' "hatchet man," someone in the game for his physicality and with the unspoken message to make his presence felt. In this regard, Loscutoff, called "Jungle Jim," came right out of Central Casting. Auerbach's philosophy was as simple and direct as a backside pick: Mess with my stars and someone else will take your head off; an eye for an eye. Such was the way Auerbach always viewed things, both on the court and off it, too.

"When I played my college ball at the University of Oregon, I led the conference in scoring and rebounding," Loscutoff would say years later. "I thought I was a pretty good rebounder and I played defense. But we had so many scorers on the Celtics that I had to change my game to the point where I just boxed out and helped Russell get rebounds, played defense, and took care of my team. I was considered a role player. Each Celtic had his role, and that's the way, more or less, that Auerbach designated us to play that role."

Loscutoff had grown up on the West Coast. When he had first

come to Boston, he hadn't liked Auerbach, considering him obnoxious, someone who treated others badly. Unlike Heinsohn, who didn't mind being one of the whipping boys and rarely took it seriously because he always knew what Auerbach was doing, Loscutoff never liked it.

In a sense, Loscutoff was emblematic of what the NBA often was in the mid-fifties. He was a tough guy who got by more on strength and being able to do the game's dirty work than on either great ability or athleticism. The league was full of them, men who set brutal picks, rebounded with their elbows out, and ended games full of bumps and bruises. But Loscutoff could make an occasional medium-range jump shot, had good fundamentals, and always understood his role. He was a valuable piece to the ensemble Auerbach had created. He fit in very well with the other starters, and he was the one for whom Ramsey usually came in when Auerbach wanted someone to jump-start the offense.

He also became a certain cult hero, thanks to Johnny Most, who began calling him "Jungle Jim." Eventually, he was profiled in *Saga*, a national men's magazine, in an article titled "Confessions of an NBA Hatchet Man," saying, "I play in a jungle where the trees swing back, and the only thing I have to protect myself is my bare fists and a jockstrap."

Now he was at the foul line in the biggest moment of his basketball life, the biggest moment in the Celtics' eleven-year history.

He was never a great free throw shooter, maybe 65 percent on a good day, and later he would remember that his hands were shaking.

No matter.

Loscutoff made the free throw with just one second left on the clock, the Celtics now leading 125–123.

———

But the Hawks weren't done yet.

Somehow it was only fitting.

This team that had been counted out back in December was still alive here on this April afternoon, even down two with just one second on the clock.

They called time-out.

The Hawks huddled around Hannum, and he came up with a last-second play, one so apparently bizarre that even decades later several of the Hawks still remembered it vividly.

His plan was to take the ball out of bounds underneath the Hawks' basket. Then he was going to throw it off the backboard at the other end of the court, a monumental feat in itself. Then Pettit was going to get the carom after it bounced off the backboard and put it in the basket, and the game would be tied again.

It was a play the Hawks used to fool around with in practice, and it worked about 50 percent of the time. It was a play Hannum had learned years earlier with the Rochester Royals.

"When Alex outlined the play in the huddle, I thought he was nuts," Martin would say later. "He couldn't spit in the ocean if he was on the beach. You stand down there and try to throw it that far. You'll throw your arm out of socket, and when he did it, Boston didn't know what the hell was happening."

No, they didn't.

Cousy later said the Celtics should have had someone guarding Hannum out of bounds, making it a more difficult pass.

But they didn't, and Hannum did just what he said he would do, throwing it the entire ninety-four feet and hitting the backboard straight on, the ball coming right back to Pettit, just as Hannum had predicted it would. But Pettit seemed to have trouble catching it as it caromed off the backboard. He seemed to almost bobble it, before throwing it back at the basket as if it were a quick touch shot. It stayed on the rim, then rolled off.

The Celtics were the NBA champions.

Finally.

The crowd rushed out on the parquet floor, engulfing the players who were both jumping around in joyous jubilation and trying to get to the runway between the benches that would take them to their locker room. It was the first championship for a Boston team in sixteen years, and even now, so many decades later, the old black-and-white photographs capture the frenzied moment, the fans running out of the stands, the players almost in a state of disbelief, many of them carried out on "shoulder rides," as one paper reported. It was one of those freeze-frame moments that later would be reenacted with future Celtics' championships, but none was ever as sweet as this one.

For this one had its roots back there in the late forties when the Celtics were little more than an afterthought on the Boston sports scene. It had its roots back there with Tony Lavelli playing "Lady of Spain" on his accordion at halftime. It had its roots back there in the "Milkman's Special" and in all those games when there were too many empty seats in the Garden, the Celtics almost an irrelevancy on the Boston sports scene. It had its roots in Brown's once not being able to give the players their play-off shares because he simply didn't have the money. It had its roots in endless trips and in too many crowded locker rooms without enough hot water. It had its roots in the eleven years of growing pains that had brought the Celtics to this wonderful moment.

No one knew, of course, that this was the start of one of the greatest teams in the history of American sport; no one knew this was the day the Celtic dynasty started. No one could know that this championship, which seemed to have taken so long, was the start of so many that would follow, or that this team would, in many ways, be the first team of basketball's modern era, the model for so many other great teams that would follow. All they knew was that this was the greatest day in the history of this fledgling franchise, the Celtics, the world champions. Let the celebration begin.

CHAPTER THIRTEEN

The Celtics' locker room was jammed with sportswriters, photographers, and anyone else who could get in the door. There were jubilant shouts and a "Heinsohn . . . Heinsohn" chant as he was lying on a trainer's table, drinking a beer, and rubbing his skinned knee, a result of being carried off the court.

"My nervous system is shot," Auerbach said. "This is a great team. The fellows refused to quit, and finally came through. This is a great day."

Years later, after all the championships, he would say that this first one had been the sweetest, that there never was another one that meant as much as this first one against the Hawks. Not surprising. This had been validation. This had been his basketball redemption. No longer was he just another crazed coach forever stomping his feet and yelling at the refs. No longer was he just another pro coach trying to survive. Never again would people in the game look at him the same way, even in Boston. After this, he always would be cheered in the Boston Garden, always respected, then adored, then revered, almost as if he had been right there with Naismith when the game had been invented, forever unchallenged. This was his slice of basketball immortality. In a sense, it was the case for all of them. Winning changed the perception of all the players, even Cousy, as famed as he was. They all were champions, something they would carry with them forever.

Auerbach started moving through the room, congratulating the players. The small room was still a mob scene, loud, raucous, complete with sportswriters jousting with one another for position. At one point he and Cousy stood in a corner, hemmed in by sportswriters.

"Here's the guy," he said, his arm around Cousy. "Here's my sidekick. He brought us this far, and the team carried through in the clincher."

They had both come so very far from that draft in 1950, back when both the NBA and the Celtics had been in such a different world, back when Cousy had been "the local yokel."

"Cousy and I have been chasing this for seven years," he continued. "My nervous system is shot. What can I say? I thought we were goners there twice and we both had the game won four or five times, but Hannum and I blew it."

He let out a big sigh.

"Fellas, it wound up okay, but you know I could have wound up an awful bum."

He was asked about Sharman's bad shooting, whether he had given any thought to taking him out.

"You go with your best," he said. "He's the tops. So he was missing. Maybe he'd get hot. I tell ya, you have to go with your best."

Cousy had had a horrible shooting game, after having such a great game in the fourth game in St. Louis, the one the Celtics simply had to win or else go down 3–1, and another one in the fifth game in the Garden, the one that had put them up 3–2. But he had missed a key free throw, and ever the perfectionist as he was, that was on his mind.

"Imagine me missing that second free throw that would have sewed it up," he said, almost to himself. "Just as I was about to shoot I started to think about how I would throw it up there and didn't follow through. A player should never think at that time. Just throw it up automatically and you won't miss."

Sharman, too, had had a brutal shooting game, so uncharacteristic for him. In the middle of the series, Hannum had called him the best middle-distance shooter in the game.

"I only had two hours sleep after we dropped that one in St. Louis," Sharman said. "Last night I kept waking up so often I only had a couple of hours more."

It had been the two rookies, Russell with his amazing 32 rebounds and 19 points, and Heinsohn with his 37 points and 23 rebounds, who, in the biggest game in the franchise's young history, had given Boston its greatest basketball moment. In retrospect, maybe that made sense. They didn't carry the baggage into the game that Cousy, Sharman, and Auerbach did. They weren't playing for all those years that had come before, either. They thought it came easy.

"I never saw such a game played by a man under such terrific pressure," Sharman said, pointing toward Heinsohn. "He bailed us out at least half a dozen times. Did you ever see another series like this one? I never did, in any sport. The mental strain was worse than the physical strain."

Then he moved over to where Heinsohn was.

"Tommy," he said, "that was a wonderful basketball game. You're really a great basketball player. Hey, Tom, give me five, boy. You and Russell. You're not rookies anymore."

"Don't you ever feel any pressure on a basketball court?" a sportswriter asked Heinsohn.

"Pressure?" he yelled. "Course I feel pressure, like everyone else. But if the shot's there. Take them. So I took them. What the deuce is a guy supposed to do with that ball? Eat it? Let them eat it if they want to."

But he hadn't played as though he had felt pressure. In fact, from the time he had joined the team in training camp, his adjustment to the NBA had been seamless. Now he arguably had been the Celtics' most effective player in the Finals. Then again, he always played with confidence. That was the lesson he had learned in high school in north Jersey when he had had that big foul shot and realized the worst that could happen was that he might miss, and he could live with that. That realization had been liberating and had given him an unshaken confidence in himself. That always had been the bedrock of his game, and it had been today, too.

The questions kept coming at him, one after another.

The Hawks had kept the door to their locker room closed to the press for forty minutes.

When the door finally opened, it was a somber team, one that knew it had come so very, very close—a call here, a play there, a game that had come down to the last second of double overtime.

The center of attention was Hannum, the coach who had put himself into the game, only to bobble the ball while looking to give it to Pettit with just seventeen seconds left in double overtime and his team only down a point, the play in which he had been called for traveling.

"Well, I say I didn't walk," he said. "I didn't have possession of the ball and I was trying to grab it. But I didn't walk.

"However," he continued, "Boston is a truly great team. Sure, Boston has great stars. But we have great spirit and we almost did it."

Yes, they did.

It had been a remarkable year for them, one that had seen them overcome a coaching change, a midseason injury to Pettit, and still come so close to winning their first NBA title. It also had been a sweet reward for Kerner, who had been so much of the NBA from the beginning, and even had gotten an apology before the game from Auerbach for the punch, an apology he graciously accepted.

Over in the Celtics' locker room, Heinsohn also was effusive in his praise for the Hawks, especially for Hagan and Pettit. Pettit had scored 39 points and grabbed 19 rebounds, even if he blamed himself for missing the last shot at the end, the shot he really never had had much of a chance on.

Cousy, who was sitting nearby, looked at Heinsohn and said, "The kid's the greatest. What pressure. And how he played under it all."

Soon afterward, Russell yelled, "Well here it is, boys."

He was talking about his goatee, which he had worn all season. He was the only player in the league with any facial hair, and he had promised to shave it off if the Celtics won the championship. Heinsohn had just shaved it off for him.

"Or, I mean there it isn't. No more goatee. It's down the drain. I promised to do it and no one can ask me about the thing anymore."

"What was that goatee all about, anyway?" asked Clif Keane.

"Well, I came here with it and somebody on the team asked, 'What's that thing, anyway?' and I told him I was going to keep right on wearing it until we won the division title. Then I decided to wear it through the play-offs. And if we lost I was going to keep it until we won the championship, no matter how long it took. But I said if we won, I'd take it off. So it's down."

He paused a beat.

"Let's see," he continued, "that's three championships in a year for me. The NCAA. The Olympics. And with these fellows."

He sat down.

But he didn't stop talking.

"I was never so scared in my life. Did I say I was scared? Man, I was shaking all over my body. See me leap out there when it was over? Felt like jumpin' all night long."

Russell had also blocked five shots, including the huge one on the Hawks' Coleman near the end of regulation, the play that probably saved the game.

"What did the Rook get?" he asked, motioning toward Heinsohn. "Thirty-seven points?"

"Hey, Rook," he yelled. "Quite a day. You're great. How many did Pettit get? Don't tell me 39. I thought I did a good job on him and he gets 39 points? Great ballplayer. I know I battled him hard and he got those points on me."

This was a different side of Russell, one the media never saw. This was the Russell his teammates sometimes saw, but only when he felt comfortable, secure in the group. And for the first time since he'd arrived in December, under a very large micro-scope, the pressure was finally off. The Celtics had won. He had done what he was supposed to do. There were no more games to play. Now he could do what all young players do in a winning locker room—revel in the moment.

Heinsohn was walking around the room, posing for pictures, doing radio interviews.

"Want to be my agent?" he asked around the room. "Sign me up, quick. I'm going for a big price."

Cousy sat in front of his locker, too tired to do anything else, trying to wipe the tears, the emotion he couldn't stop, out of his eyes. He had been so exhausted after the fourth game in the series, the one in which he had lost a false tooth, that he almost hadn't been able to walk up the stairs to the dressing room in Kiel Auditorium. He had been so tired that he hadn't taken part in the postgame celebration. Now he had played all but seven seconds of the fifty-eight-minute game. He didn't even remember getting back to the locker from the jubilant court and the frenzied crowd. Now he was emotionally drained, in the middle of a joyous celebration, and all he could think of was of the long journey it had taken to get to this moment—all those train rides; all those nights in those crummy little locker rooms in those early years when the Celtics had been so very far from an NBA title; all those nights when there had been too little hot water in the showers, and too few fans in the seats; all those years of all those big, empty arenas where the glamour always was somewhere else.

"We finally did it," he said, almost to himself.

It had been only a handful of years since Brown had mortgaged his house to keep the team afloat, only a few years since Auerbach always was trying to educate both the sportswriters and the fans to what pro basketball was about, back when it so often seemed as if the Celtics always were playing to the sound of one hand clapping. They still might not be able to outdraw the Bruins, or even come close to competing in popularity with the Red Sox, but they were the best team in basketball, and no one could ever take that away from them.

The irony was that both he and Sharman had had horrible shooting games, 5 for 40 between the two of them, these two men who carried the Celtics for so many years now, if always falling short once the play-offs started.

Yet wasn't that the answer, too?

Wasn't that the reason why the Celtics were now the NBA champions?

They didn't need Cousy and Sharman to be supermen in black sneakers every night anymore to be a great team. Others could bail them out, as both Heinsohn and Russell had done. Or like Ramsey, who had 10 of these 16 points in the two overtimes. Others could chip in, such as Risen, the old vet who had been so kind to Russell when he had first arrived. He had had 16 points coming off the bench. Jack Nichols had had 8 points off the bench. Andy Phillip had had 5. The three old veterans had come up big in the biggest game.

Hadn't that always been Auerbach's vision, a team where everyone knew their roles? Hadn't that always had been the way he set out to create his team, not always necessarily the best players, but a roster full of guys who understood why they were there, who understood why some teams won and some teams didn't? It was what Auerbach always had known, the philosophy that later would be recognized as Celtics basketball as the players came and went but the titles kept coming; it was the one constant through the years, the feeling that the Celtics always were a team in the best sense of the word.

Eventually, it would become known as the "Celtic Mystique" as

the titles kept coming and there always seemed to be another banner going up in the rafters. The "Celtic Mystique" was that sense
that somehow the Celtics would find a way to win—a leprechaun
would come down from the rafters, the other team would get a bad
bounce off the parquet floor, some old ghost would come out of the
misty past and cause some opponent's mistake, something. That
was "the Celtic Mystique," the sense that they were somehow different, the sense that they had some secret formula no other franchise had, the reason why all those banners were staring down
from the rafters, that indefinable something that made the Celtics
the Celtics.

Later, it also would be called "Celtic Pride," but whatever it
was, it had started on this April afternoon in '57.

It started with this first championship.

It started with the public validation of Auerbach's vision for
his basketball team.

Wasn't that always what he had preached, even in those years
when few had listened, when he had seemed like a minister with
no congregation, even back in those early years when the local
sportswriters thought he was loud and obnoxious, little more than
a salesman with a sample case they had no interest in buying?
Wasn't that why he always made his team stand up during time-
outs while the other teams always seemed to sit? Wasn't that why
he always made them wear jackets and ties on the road? Wasn't
that why they could have mixed drinks on the road? Weren't these
among all those little signs that told people the Celtics were different, the Celtics were special?

Hadn't it always been about his vision, even if too few people
ever knew what he was talking about, this vision he first had when
he initially set out to coach the Washington Capitols in the new

league to which no one knew what was going to happen, the vision that dictated that if he were going to fail, at least he would fail doing things his way? Hadn't that always been what he had seen, even back there when no one else had seen it—other coaches, referees, the damned sportswriters, every damned one of them?

His vision.

Because for all of them on this afternoon in the Boston Garden, this afternoon that would always be a piece of Boston sports history, he had chased this moment the longest, all the way from the tenement world of his Brooklyn boyhood, that Depression world he always carried with him wherever the bouncing ball took him. He had chased it through all those old train rides through those bleak towns back in the Tri-Cities. He had chased it all those lonely nights in his suite in the Hotel Lenox while eating his Chinese food, all those nights on the road alone in some hotel room, getting ready to play another game, always another game. He had chased the game his entire life, always trying to run up the mountain, only to always see more mountain, and here he finally was at the top of this world he long ago had created for himself.

Years later, he would say that throughout that summer, the enormity of what he'd done would suddenly hit him. He was the coach of the world champion Boston Celtics. He was the coach of the world champions—Arnold Auerbach, Hymie's son. He was Arnold Auerbach, who had grown up in a Brooklyn ghetto. He was Arnold Auerbach, who had had to fight for everything he had achieved in his life, as if his fighting the referees was a metaphor for how he always had viewed the world. He was Arnold Auerbach, who coached the best team in the world.

But now, in the jubilant locker room, the game was over, the celebration was over, and he was coming down from the emotion. At one point he was talking into two tape recorders and puffing on his signature cigar in between quotes.

Earlier, he had been thrown in the shower by Heinsohn and Loscutoff, cigar and all.

"We've been chasing this for seven years," a drenched Auerbach said as he changed into a sweat suit for the drive back across the city to his hotel.

But he was wrong about that.

The Celtics had been chasing it for seven years.

Auerbach had been chasing it his entire life.

The next day the *Globe* had the story of the Celtics' winning their first NBA title on the front page of the Sunday paper, right there with a new column by Kay Furcolo, wife of Massachusetts governor Foster Furcolo, on how she spent her days, and a story on how mail was piling up in post offices and how the country's postmaster general should be fired for halting Saturday mail delivery. All these stories were eclipsed by a banner headline in big bold type that said, SHAKY JORDAN REGIME RULED BY FOE OF U.S., about how Syria had reinforced its army in Jordan.

"The Celtics, after an 11-year wait, pushed the blood pressure of 13,909 rooters to the bursting point before edging the St. Louis Hawks 125–123 in a double overtime thriller yesterday afternoon at the Garden to win their first National Basketball Association championship," the game story began.

It was written, appropriately enough, by Jack Barry, the man who had liked both Auerbach and professional basketball from the beginning, back when to do so was to be in a lonely place.

There also were two pictures on the front page. The first showed Heinsohn kneeling down in front of Auerbach and the Celtics' bench in the game's closing seconds. His face buried in a towel, he was unable to look. The second showed both Auerbach and Heinsohn, now standing up, as they first realized Pettit's shot had missed and the Celtics had won.

Inside, there were more pictures, including one of Heinsohn being carried off the court, and four of Russell jumping all around the court seconds after the game ended, all his pent-up emotion unleashed. There also were five pictures of Red Sox pitcher Frank Sullivan, wearing a dark sport jacket. Showing him in varying stages of emotional distress, the photos were under a headline, FRANK SULLIVAN SPENDS A RELAXING DAY OFF.

There had been a sidebar story on Ramsey, saying how he had carried the Celtics in the first overtime, and how he had left the locker room celebration early because he had to get back to Fort Knox in Kentucky to get his army discharge. Having joined the Celtics in early January after missing the entire 1955–56 season, he had been traveling back and forth to Kentucky ever since, trying to squeeze in games in these last few months as a soldier in the United States Army, to the point that during the play-offs, one wire service story had referred to him as Frank Ramsey of the United States Army.

"That Hagan gave us fits, didn't he?" Ramsey said of his old college teammate and Kentucky high school nemesis who had scored 24 points for the Hawks. "He can't be ignored for a second. Works like a cat and is as strong as a lion. He's going to be heard from in this league."

Another headline said, CELTICS' TRIUMPH RATES WITH BOSTON'S TOP THRILLS. The article, written by Jerry Nason, said, "More than

13,909 fans left the Garden yesterday convinced they had witnessed one of the most exciting sports episodes in this city in the past 25 years."

Nason went on to say the championship game was being rated with such unforgettable thrills as Mel Hill's "sudden death" goal that won the Stanley Cup for the Bruins in 1939; Boston College's Sugar Bowl victory over Georgetown in Fenway Park in the forties, called by Grantland Rice "the most exciting college football game ever played"; the Boston Braves' Johnny Sain's outlasting Bob Feller in the opening game of the '48 World Series at Braves Field; and Sandy Saddler's knocking out Tommy Collins in the Garden on St. Patrick's night in 1952.

There also was the box score.

It said how five Celtics—Heinsohn, Russell, Risen, Ramsey, and Cousy—had finished in double figures, compared to four for the Hawks—Pettit, Hagan, Martin, and Coleman.

Above the box score it said, TOMORROW: BASEBALL.

There was no celebration in downtown Boston. There was no parade through the streets. There was nothing.

Three days later, many of the Celtics were in Des Moines, Iowa. It was the beginning of a seventeen-game tour against a team called the Professional All-Stars, comprising NBA players.

Why?

For the money.

"There was a promoter in Boston," Cousy said. "He arranged it, we could make a few bucks, and it was fun. No pressure."

Russell had left the day after the final game to drive the 1,324 miles to Des Moines, part of his plan to drive across the country, eventually ending in San Francisco, where he was going to leave his new car and continue the tour. The trip to Des Moines took twenty-three hours, and after the Celtics beat the All-Stars 103–102, he got back in the car and drove over the Rocky Mountains to Denver. Eventually, the tour made its way to Los Angeles. It had been the first time Cousy had ever been there, and one night he and Sharman went out to a nightclub where he was introduced to Walter Winchell, the famous gossip columnist who was syndicated in two thousand newspapers around the country and supposedly was read by fifty million people.

The Celtics' tour usually got a paragraph in the Boston sports pages.

The more important Celtics news that week following the title game was the Celtics' selecting a little-known college player from a small black college called North Carolina State in the NBA Draft. His name was Sam Jones, and he was listed as a six-foot-four forward. Because they had won the title, they had the eighth and last pick in the first round, and one Boston paper had already told fans not to expect a whole lot because there weren't eight quality players in the entire draft.

"A Boston spokesman said that Jones was recommended by one source as 'the best in the entire South' this season while playing with the all-Negro college," an Associated Press story said.

There were eleven rounds in the draft, but only Jones would go on to make the team the following year. Later, it would become known that Jones had been recommended by Bones McKinney, the coach at Wake Forest, who had played for Auerbach in Washington, as Auerbach had never seen Jones play. Once again, as they had with the acquisition of Russell, Auerbach and the Celtics had benefited from his past associations and his trust in their judgment. Sam Jones would go on to become a Hall of Fame player for the Celtics, and eventually he would team in the Celtics backcourt with K. C. Jones, the two becoming known as the "Jones Boys."

The first pick in the NBA Draft had been "Hot Rod" Hundley, a flashy ballhandling guard from West Virginia, who had been taken by the Minneapolis Lakers after they had obtained the first pick from the Cincinnati Royals by giving up veterans Clyde Lovellette and Jim Paxson.

The drafting of Jones did not get a lot of play in the Boston sports pages. No one had ever heard of him, he didn't come from a big-time college program, and basketball season was over, right? The big story of the day in Boston, though, was not the addition of Sam Jones to the Celtics, but the prospect of the Red Sox home opener against the Yankees at Fenway Park. Frank Sullivan was scheduled to start for the Sox and Johnny Kucks for the Yankees. A thumbnail ad in the *Boston Daily Globe* said:

> The Yanks are coming. What a show—Ted Williams, Jimmy Piersall, Jackie Jensen, Dick Gernert are ready to slug it out with the big guns of the World Champions— Mickey Mantle, Yogi Berra, Hank Bauer and Bill Skowron.

Tickets were $2.75 for box seats, $1.40 for the grandstand, and you could sit in the bleachers for $.75. The opening day ceremonies were going to feature the Harvard Band.

It was one more reminder that Boston was all about the Red Sox, even in the wake of the city's first championship in sixteen years. The Celtics had won the NBA title, the Garden had been sold out, people had rushed the court, and there had been headlines in the newspapers the next day, but now that was all gone, almost as if it had never happened. Now the season was over and sports in Boston were back to the way they always had been, all eyes back on the Red Sox.

There also was a small newspaper story that said how five thousand people had met the Hawks at the St. Louis airport on their return from Boston, showing them a tremendous outpouring of affection.

But the Celtics?

The Celtics' season was over.

But its legacy would remain in ways unfathomable at the time.

If nothing else, it was the beginning of the Celtics' dynasty, the greatest in American sport. It forever changed the perception of Auerbach from just another abrasive coach fighting with the referees into a basketball visionary, someone who could both build and manage a team better than anyone else on the planet, the first step in his basketball immortality. It cemented Cousy's reputation as the archetype of the creative point guard, the one against which all the creative ones that came after him forever would be measured.

It also was the first step in Russell's incredible professional career that would eventually see him being called the greatest winner in the history of American sport. And if you looked close enough, you could see him as the first pioneer in basketball's evolution, the first man who turned defense into an art form, the first big man as a great athlete, too, the prototype of the modern big man. In so many ways he was a generation ahead of himself, as an athlete and an activist, too; he was a preview of what was to come in the years ahead, a towering presence.

There also was the sense that this afternoon in April '57 had ushered in the modern NBA, courtesy of both national television and the game's having been so compelling, the sense that a Maginot Line in the game's history was crossed that afternoon, and afterward there was no turning back. There would be more and more black players. There would be more and more interest in the NBA. There would be an America about to change right in front of us, and the NBA, with its emerging black stars, would be a part of that change.

EPILOGUE

The same two teams met in the NBA Finals the next year, only this time Russell tore the tendons in his ankle in the third game, and he didn't come back until the sixth game, the last game of the series.

The clincher had been in Kiel Auditorium, a game in which Pettit scored 50 points and the Kiel crowd rushed the court, a similar scene to what had happened in the Garden the year before.

The excitement for the Hawks in St. Louis, which had begun the year before when the Hawks averaged more than ten thousand spectators a game, had carried over to the 1957–58 season. Their first game, featured in a banner headline in the *St. Louis Globe-Democrat* newspaper, sold out. There had been so much interest in the series in St. Louis that Kerner had installed a closed circuit in the Kiel Opera House on the other side of the gymnasium floor so that an extra thirty-five hundred fans could watch the game.

It was all one more example of the growth of the NBA.

The Celtics had taken the Hawks to six games, without Russell for two of the games, and with an injured Russell in the last one. The Celtics all believed they would have won if Russell hadn't gotten hurt. But for Kerner, the title was his sweet validation, his trip to the top of the mountain, one that had taken so many years and so much hustling, so very far from the Tri-Cities.

Never again would the Hawks win another title, even though Pettit would go on to become one of the NBA's all-time great players before retiring in 1965 to go back home to Louisiana to work for a bank. By then, all of the Hawks who had been in the '57 Finals were out of the game. And in 1968, Kerner was once again beset by money problems. He was being challenged at the gate by a new NHL hockey team in St. Louis. Unable to find any moneyed people in St. Louis willing to buy the team and no doubt worn down by all his years in the game, Kerner sold the Hawks to a group of men from Atlanta. They moved the franchise to Atlanta and renamed them the Atlanta Hawks, who could trace their roots back to the Tri-Cities when they had been the Blackhawks. Never again would the NBA return to St. Louis.

The Celtics came back to win again in 1959, sweeping the Minneapolis Lakers. The core of the team was the same—Cousy, Sharman, Russell, Heinsohn, Ramsey, Loscutoff. Sam Jones had been added following the '57 season, and from the beginning it was apparent he was another Auerbach steal; someone who would become one of the best shooting guards in the game; someone who would become a Hall of Fame player and further cement Auerbach's growing reputation as a great talent scout; someone who was a step ahead.

K. C. Jones, drafted by the Celtics in the spring of '56, joined the team after two years in the army. Russell's college teammate at the University of San Francisco, he was a tough, tenacious defender, now, too, in the Hall of Fame. This gave the Celtics three black players, one more telling example that Auerbach's sole intent was to make his team better, regardless of the social repercussions. Then again, Cousy always had said that Auerbach never saw race, only basketball players. It also made Russell feel more comfortable on the Celtics, as he got along with both K. C. and Sam Jones.

The Jones Boys, as they came to be called in those early years, would come off the bench to spell Cousy and Sharman, changing the Celtics. They were both younger and more athletic, and they invariably would pick up opposing guards in the backcourt, applying defensive pressure and making the Celtics better defensively. It was one more example of Auerbach's use of his bench to give opposing teams a different look, and in this case he had the best of both worlds, the offensive brilliance of Cousy and Sharman, juxtaposed with young legs and defensive pressure of the Jones Boys.

They won again in 1960, beating the Hawks in seven games, the Hawks coached by Macauley.

They won again in 1961, beating the Hawks in five games, aided by rookie Tom "Satch" Sanders, a willowy six-foot-six defensive specialist from NYU. Auerbach called it the greatest team ever assembled, and he might have been right. Certainly it was the deepest.

They won again in 1962, beating the Lakers in seven games.

They won again in 1963 in Cousy's last year, beating the Lakers in a seventh game in Los Angeles.

The Celtics were changing, now different than the team that had won in '57. Sharman had retired after the '61 season, and now Cousy was gone, too, feted in April in an emotional farewell ceremony in Boston Garden, at the time the biggest ever for a Boston athlete and one highlighted by a telegram from President Kennedy. Near the end, surrounded by his wife and two young daughters and standing in the middle of the parquet floor, Cousy was in tears. As he struggled to control his emotions, in the stillness of the Garden, a fan's loud voice came rolling down from the second balcony, cutting through the building. "We love ya, Cooz."

You didn't need a press release to know an era had ended. Cousy, "Mr. Basketball," had been the public face of the Celtics for so long. Now he was leaving to become the coach at nearby Boston College.

But the Celtics kept rolling along, winning again in '64, the last season for both Ramsey and Loscutoff.

The season before, the Celtics became the first team in NBA history to start five black players in a game—Russell, the Jones Boys, Sanders, and Willie Naulls, who had come over in a trade before the season. It happened during the time when Heinsohn had been hurt. But it was symbolic, even if Auerbach and the players never made a big deal of it, save for the time in the early days when Ramsey had been the only white Celtic player on the court and Russell had looked over at him and quipped, "Hey, Frank, we've got you outnumbered."

That September, when Walter Brown died of a heart attack at his Cape Cod summer home, an era ended in Boston.

The Celtics won again in 1965, the last year for Heinsohn.

Auerbach retired from coaching after the '66 season and another title, their eighth in a row and ninth in the past ten years. After the clinching game, he and a New York writer friend, Milton Gross, had gone back to Auerbach's suite at the Hotel Lenox. Gross worked for the *New York Post*, the so-called liberal paper in

New York. He had sat with Auerbach and Russell shortly after Russell had arrived in Boston in December '56 before he had even played a game. Auerbach had wanted Russell to sit with him and watch an NBA game from up close, and Gross had done a column on it. Now it was almost a decade later. No one back in late December '56 ever could have envisioned Auerbach trying to give a young rookie a crash course in the NBA. Now, so many titles later, Gross was in Boston to do a column on Auerbach's last game.

Auerbach ordered Chinese food over the phone, then barked at the person taking the order. "Auerbach. Who the hell do you think it is? And hurry. I'm starving."

He started to make some French fries.

"What if you had lost this one?" Gross asked. "Would you have cried?

"Cry? I don't know," Auerbach said. "I might cry later, anyway. I've fulfilled my life in basketball. Now why don't you get out of here and leave me alone?"

He made Russell the coach, for as he said, "We're like a family. It wouldn't be easy bringing in someone from outside the family to be part of the family. Russell can do the job."

The Celtics lost in the Eastern Conference finals to Chamberlain and Philadelphia in 1967, then came back and won two more titles before Russell decided he'd had enough. He was replaced as coach by Heinsohn, Auerbach once again keeping things in the family.

But the Celtics' dynasty was over.

The scorecard said they had won eleven NBA titles in thirteen years, the greatest run in the history of American professional sports.

But the Celtics had accomplished more than just the eleven

titles. They had ushered in the modern era of the NBA. They had been the team that had taken the NBA from its dance hall past, from the time when professional basketball all too often seemed to be on the same dance card with roller derby, into the game we know today. They were the bridge. They were the visionaries, encompassing everything from style of play, to coaching, to a standard of excellence against which all the NBA teams to follow would be judged. After Auerbach, never again would an NBA coach be viewed as essentially meaningless, little more than baggage on the bench. The NBA would continue to grow, continue to evolve, spreading across the country, a true national league, its superstars walking alongside the other kings of American sport.

And ultimately, the Celtics of that era achieved their basketball immortality, both individually and collectively.

Auerbach would become universally recognized as the greatest coach in NBA history, one of the game's seminal figures. Forgotten would be his feuding with referees, his verbal sparring with sportswriters, the abrasive side of his personality. Remembered would be his shrewdness, his ability to both evaluate talent and motivate it. Also remembered would be his titles, his incredible coaching resume that became his legend. Auerbach would be remembered as the man who built the greatest dynasty in American sport virtually by himself, the one constant through all the years as the players came and went and everything changed except him.

"It was all him," Cousy often said. "He was the Celtic Mystique."

Auerbach would be remembered as the Celtic patriarch, morphing into the role of general manager, then president, and in the end seemingly becoming as much a part of Boston as the Kennedys and Paul Revere's ride, complete with a statue outside Faneuil Hall to prove it.

He also would be seen as a racial pioneer, though that never had been his intention. He had been all about winning; if black players could help him do so, so be it. But if being the first NBA coach to start five black players in a game back in '63 had been the right coaching move at the time, it had taken a certain courage to do that, too. Then again, Auerbach always had the courage of his convictions, even in those early years of his career when that hurt him, and even during the sixties when the Celtics, although the best team in the world, rarely filled the Garden, usually averaging only around eight thousand for regular season games, and always being outdrawn by the Bruins, even though the Bruins back then were mediocre at best.

Was it simply the issue of race, a product of a certain time and place in Boston, and a pro game that was changing in front of everyone, as if it mirrored the civil rights movement, bringing both change and the reaction to it?

Was it a certain backlash to Russell's public persona in Boston, and his increasingly militant public stance, the sense that Boston's basketball star was often not outwardly likeable, at least to the so-called white dollars that kept the league afloat? Had Eddie Gottlieb been right in the early fifties, when he warned that white people weren't going to pay to see too many Negroes play basketball, unless they were the Globetrotters?

Was it merely one more symbolic reminder that Boston still wasn't a very good basketball town, and never had been?

Was it a combination of all these things?

This is the great unanswered question of the era.

Certainly, it was a combination of many things. Change never comes easy, and America in the sixties was all about change, with generations in collision, and the civil rights movement, too. There was little question Russell was a polarizing figure, and his increasing militancy obviously was at odds in a city that would have its racial epiphany in September 1974 when court-ordered school busing started and tore the city apart. Then there was the reality back then that in its heart of hearts Boston was a hockey town, regardless of how good the Celtics were.

"I don't think Boston really caught on to the Celtics until the Bird Era," Cousy recently said.

By then the NBA had exploded nationally thanks to the popularity of Bird and Magic Johnson.

And, oh yeah, Bird was white.

Race in Boston has always been complicated.

Cousy would go on to be remembered as one of the game's all-time greats, remembered as someone who had helped save the league in those early years. He later coached the Cincinnati Royals for a few years in the early seventies. He was one of the few players from that era to retain his celebrity for the rest of his life, especially in New England where everyone knew Bob Cousy, even those who never saw him play and couldn't tell you anything about basketball. For years he was the colored man on the Celtics' TV broadcasts, working with Heinsohn, as if nothing had really changed since all those days when they used to ride into Boston from Worcester together. But it was more than that. To many people of a certain age, Cousy was the Celtics, and he always would be.

Russell would be known as the greatest winner in the history of American sport, even if for years his relationship with the city of Boston became as complicated as two old lovers who didn't deal with each other anymore. His complicated rivalry-friendship with Chamberlain came, in many ways, to define the era. They were the

two most towering figures in the game, these two unique, icono-
clastic, proud, black men, whose personal battles on the court
elevated the entire sport. They also were products of a changing
country, two sports superstars, both very different, but so linked
together by their race, their size, their notoriety, two black athletes
who spoke to the future, not the past.

Russell retired after the '69 season as the player-coach, even
after a season that had seen the Celtics all but limp into the play-
offs, and Russell spent much of the season looking old and basically
uninterested.

Yet they still won.

Then he went off to be Bill Russell. He spent time in Holly-
wood for a while. He got divorced. He wore dashikis. He spoke
out about racism. He got remarried. He got divorced again. In
1975 he refused to be inducted into the Basketball Hall of Fame,
though he would have been the first black to be inducted. He
coached the Sacramento Kings for a time. He wrote a thoughtful,
reflective memoir called *Second Wind*. He supposedly was a re-
cluse for a while, living on Washington State's Mercer Island.

In the early years of the new millennium, he began showing up periodically in the FleetCenter in ways he never had before. Auerbach always sat about ten rows up at midcourt, across
from the visitor's bench, and on those nights when Auerbach was
there, Russell always sat one row behind him, spending the game
hunched over, as if always talking to Auerbach, these two old warriors in the twilight, so far from that first season in '57. In 2009
he wrote the beautiful little book *Red and Me*, an affectionate
look at a relationship that had begun amidst so much uncertainty
and tension in December '56 and had evolved over time into a
deep friendship.

Later, as the decades went by, and so many of the particulars were forgotten, he, too, became beloved in Boston in ways he never had been as a player. So much time had passed. So much history had come and gone. The country was such a different place than it had been when Russell had been a player. So many people had come and gone. So many of the old battles had been fought and were now just memories, stories in old books. The signature moment was in 1999 when his number, raised to the rafters in the early seventies in a private ceremony with just a few of his old teammates present because he didn't want a public one, was reraised into the rafters before an adoring crowd.

That was the ceremony where Bill Cosby and Bryant Gumbel were the emcees, and ten thousand people had bought tickets. He was in Boston as part of his National Mentoring Partnership, which had become his passion, and longtime recording star Johnny Mathis, whom he had known in college so many years earlier, sang. Auerbach, then eighty-one, was there, complete with his ever-present cigar. Cousy, Heinsohn, and former Celtics great John Havlicek, who had joined the team in 1962, all spoke.

That had been the night so many of those old ghosts of the past were buried forever.

In many ways, Russell is appreciated now more in memory than he was when he was playing, as people tend to view the game differently now. They have more of an appreciation for his rebounding, his defensive innovations, the way he changed the game. Plus, he's now a mythic figure, in the twilight of his years, so many of the old battles either gone or forgotten, and Boston now a different place in so many ways.

I think of that often when I go to Celtics games now; I think of how no one could have made up the Celtics' story, and how very fortunate I was to have been old enough to remember that first title.

I had just turned twelve that April of '57, the perfect age to fall in love with a basketball team. Over the next few years I saw them when they played a few times in the old Providence Auditorium on North Main. We often sat in one of the rows behind the basket, yelling at the opposing players. It was never crowded, the seats were just a few bucks, and one night I saw Russell deck Jim Krebs of the Lakers, one punch at half-court.

Did we know what we had back then—a chance to see the best team in the world right up close?

Of course not.

In one of my first years as a sportswriter at the *Providence Journal*, I went to Boston to do a magazine story on Red Auerbach. It was the mid-eighties, and he was about to retire as general manager. I walked into his office. He put a timer on his desk and wound it. He then told me a zillion stories, all the while walking around his office, which was a shrine to his past. In the middle of one of these stories, the timer went off.

"That's it," he said in midstory. "I've got to watch the program."

The program?

"I watch *Hawaii Five-O* every day at four o'clock," he said.

Vintage Red.

Watching *Hawaii Five-O* reruns every day at four o'clock somehow seemed only fitting.

And as the years have gone by, and other great NBA teams have come and gone, what the Celtics of the fifties and sixties accomplished has only become more mythic; it was a time of excellence that never again can be replicated. To look at those banners that hang in the new Garden in Boston, adjacent to where the old one was, to see all those years immortalized, is almost like looking at the history of the NBA and professional basketball, too. The story of the Celtics is told in green banners hanging from the rafters in a kind of living memorial to all those old ghosts staring down on today's NBA.

But it all started on that April afternoon in '57 when the Celtics beat the Hawks in double overtime in one of the greatest games in NBA history. Back when Russell was a rookie and the only black player in the game, back when no one could have known what his legacy would be, including him . . .

That day the Celtic dynasty started.

That day the NBA became major-league.

That day was a sneak preview of a new America, of a game that included not only a black rookie who would go on to become an iconic figure in basketball history, but also the promise of a country about to go through transformational change, on the basketball court, and in the streets, too. That day, when viewed through the prism of history, was a certain demarcation line.

It was the first banner.

The one that changed everything.

NOTES

The best book I found on the St. Louis Hawks of the era is *Full Court: The Untold Stories of the St. Louis Hawks* by Greg Marecek, an in-depth view of the city, owner Ben Kerner, the players, and how a big game in Kiel Auditorium felt.

There are many books that deal with the terrain of the Celtics in the late fifties including *Red Auerbach: An Autobiography*, with Joe Fitzgerald; two books by Dan Shaughnessy, *Ever Green* and *Seeing Red*; Joe Fitzgerald's *That Championship Feeling*; Jeff Greenfield's *The World's Greatest Team*; and all the Russell books including his latest, *Red and Me*.

Anyone looking for Celtics history should check out *The Picture History of the Boston Celtics* by George Sullivan, Peter Bjarkman's *Boston Celtics Encyclopedia*, Tom Heinsohn's *Don't You Ever Smile?* and *Dynasty's End* by Thomas J. Whalen.

For the overall history of the early days of the NBA, I found Leonard Koppett's *24 Seconds to Shoot* of great value, and for a history of black players in professional basketball, I found Ron

Thomas's *They Cleared the Lane* very helpful. There's no better book on the fifties than David Halberstam's *The Fifties*.

I also relied heavily on newspaper accounts from the *Boston Globe*, both daily and evening editions, the *Boston Herald*, the *Boston Record American*, and the *Boston Sunday Advertiser*, plus several stories on Kerner from the online Sports Illustrated Vault, and *Sport* magazine articles on both Russell and Bob Pettit. I was also aided by interviews at various times with Auerbach, Russell, Heinsohn, Macauley, and Ramsey, and by doing a previous book with Cousy.

BIBLIOGRAPHY

Auerbach, Arnold "Red," and Joe Fitzgerald. *Red Auerbach: An Autobiography*. New York: G.P. Putnam's Sons, 1977.

Auerbach, Red, with Ken Dooley. *MBA Management by Auerbach: Management Tips from the Leader of One of America's Most Successful Organizations*. New York: A Wellington Press Book. Macmillan. 1991.

Bjarkman, Peter C. *Boston Celtics Encyclopedia*. Chicago: Sports Publishing, 2002.

Carey, Mike, with Jamie Most. *High Above Courtside: The Lost Memoirs of Johnny Most*. Chicago: Sports Publishing, 2002.

Cohen, Stanley. *The Game They Played*. New York: Farrar, Straus, and Giroux, 1977.

Connolly, Michael. *Rebound: Basketball, Busing, Larry Bird, and the Rebirth of Boston*. Minneapolis: Voyageur Press, 2008.

BIBLIOGRAPHY

Cousy, Bob, with Al Hirshberg. *Basketball Is My Life*. Englewood Cliffs, NJ: Prentice Hall, 1957.

Cousy, Bob, with Bob Ryan. *Cousy on the Celtic Mystique*. New York: McGraw-Hill, 1988.

Fitzgerald, Joe. *That Championship Feeling: The Story of the Boston Celtics*. New York: Charles Scribner's Sons, 1975.

Gowdy, Curt, with John Powers. *Seasons to Remember: The Way It Was in American Sport from 1954–1961*. New York: Harper-Collins, 1993.

Greenfield, Jeff. *The World's Greatest Team: A Portrait of the Boston Celtics.1957–69*. New York: A Sport Magazine Book, Random House, 1976.

Halberstam, David. *The Fifties*. New York: Fawcett Columbine, 1993.

Heinsohn, Tommy and Joe Fitzgerald. *Give 'Em the Hook*. New York: Prentice Hall, 1988.

Heinsohn, Tommy, with Leonard Lewin. *Heinsohn, Don't You Ever Smile?* Garden City, NY: Doubleday and Company, 1976.

Koppet, Leonard. *24 Seconds to Shoot: The Birth and Improbable Rise of the NBA*. Kingston, NY: Total Sports Illustrated Classics, 1968.

Marecek, Greg. *Full Court: The Untold Stories of the St. Louis Hawks*. St. Louis: Reedy Press, 2006.

Montville, Leigh. *Ted Williams: The Biography of an American Hero*. New York: Broadway Books, 2004.

BIBLIOGRAPHY

Pluto, Terry. *Tall Tales: The Glory Years of the NBA, in the Words of the Men Who Played, Coached, and Built Professional Basketball*. New York: Simon & Schuster, 1992.

Reynolds, Bill. *Cousy: His Life, Career, and the Birth of Big-Time Basketball*. New York: Simon & Schuster, 2005.

Russell, Bill. *Second Wind: The Memoirs of an Opinionated Man*. New York: Simon & Schuster, 1979.

Russell, Bill, as told to William McSweeney. *Go Up for Glory*. New York: Coward, McCann & Geoghegan, 1966.

Russell, Bill, with Alan Steinberg. *Red and Me: My Coach, My Lifelong Friend*. New York: HarperCollins, 2009.

Salzberg, Charles. *From Set Shot to Slam Dunk: The Glory Days of Basketball in the Words of Those Who Played It*. New York: E. P. Dutton, 1987.

Shaughnessy, Dan. *Ever Green: The Boston Celtics*. New York: St. Martin's Press, 1990.

Shaughnessy, Dan. *Seeing Red*. New York: Crown Publishers, 1994.

Sullivan, George. *The Picture History of the Boston Celtics*. Indianapolis: The Bobbs-Merrill Company, 1981.

Taylor, John. *The Rivalry: Bill Russell, Wilt Chamberlain, and the Golden Age of Basketball*. New York: Random House, 2005.

ACKNOWLEDGMENTS

Great editors make books better, and I am very fortunate to have a great one in Mark Chait, who not only made this a better book, but also showed kindness and compassion in dealing with the manuscript at a time when I needed both.

His assistant, Talia Platz, also greatly aided this book, with her sharp insights and expertise.

David Vigliano has been my agent for more than two decades, and never steers me wrong. I value his loyalty, his expertise, and his keen understanding of an ever-changing business.

Like any great player, Liz Abbott always comes through in the clutch, and she did it again with both her research skills and dealing with the pictures. Isabelle Brogna, semiresident wizard, once again did what I can't do, and Giuliana Brogna also provided valuable research at a time when I truly needed her help. They all have my enduring thanks.